# *Hebrew Bible*

# Book of
# Exodus

*Five books of Moses*

**SimchatChaim.com**

There is no known book without mistakes. Therefore, I ask in every language of application if anyone has any questions, comments, clarifications, corrections, please send to: simchatchaim@yahoo.com

All material used in this section may not be used for commercial purposes, but only for study and teaching.

To get this book or books and information Email me at:

simchatchaim@yahoo.com



מהדורה שניה תשפ"ד
Second edition 2024

# The contents of the book

# Introduction to the

# Jewish Bible

First you need to know that the Bible was originally written in the holy language, which today is called Hebrew.

The Tanach itself went through a series of translations from language to language until today's English language.

As a whole, the Tanakh was translated from the holy language into Greek, and from Greek into Latin, and from there into the ancient Agalic, and then into the more modern English.

The problem is when translating from language to language the original meaning is lost.

In the translation of languages there is no realistic possibility to make a completely accurate translation, since in every language there are several translation options for most words, and each word has a different connotation, and also differs to a certain extent from the exact connotation of the original word in the source language.

For example, it is possible to translate the word - **שמים**. **sky** into English for Sky and Heaven. Two suitable options that each have a different meaning from the other, and also slightly different from the full connotation of the word **sky שמים**. For this reason, along with the attempt to bridge the cultural difference, every translation is actually also an interpretation. In many cases, the translators took the approach of **extensive translation**, in which the translation adds details and interpretations beyond the original text, changes the content, and describes what is happening in a way that is more suitable to the cultural concepts accepted for the period and region. In the common translations these changes are found - to a certain degree of change - in tens of percent of the verses. The general public in these periods knew the Bible only from the translations, and therefore in different regions they actually knew different versions of the same texts, according to the local halachic belief.

The most classic example of this is this:
In the book of Exodus chapter 34 verse 29 it is explained that - KARAN [קרן] the skin of Moses face.

The word KARAN [קרן] has at least two meanings:
**A.** Radiant.
**B.** A horn, like that of a bull.
There are other meanings to this word that do not belong to this introduction.

An incorrect translation of the Book of Exodus by Jerome [the Vulgate] into Latin led to an error in the interpretation of the phrase - The horn of the skin of his face. [Exodus 34:29]. And because of this, in

Renaissance sculptures, Moses's forehead was added **Horns**.

And this is the verse in its entirety according to our translation [compare it to your Bible] - So Moses came down from Mount Sinai. And as Moses came down from the mountain bearing the two tablets of the Pact, Moses was not aware that the skin of his face was **radiant**, since he had spoken with God.

It is known that Hebrew has a vowel for every word. And there can be a word that has a different vowel from the same word. For example, the word with four letters - מ.ד.ב.ר.

מְדַבֵּר - speaker.

מִדְבָּר - desert.

מֵדְבֵּר - A speaking man.

מִדָּבָר - out of nothing.

מְדֻבָּר - thing that is being discussed.

There are **only** five vowels with the same word, and really this word has 25 vowel types!!!! which can change the entire meaning of the verse and the translation.

The first translations of the Bible were created by Jews at the beginning of the first millennium AD. During this period, most Jews gradually stopped using the Hebrew language, especially biblical Hebrew. A translated Bible became a basic necessity for the reading of the Torah in the synagogues, which was performed by two people - one who read the verse is in the original language, and an interpreter repeats his words in the spoken language.

The first translations of the Bible were created by Jews at the beginning of the first millennium AD. During this period, most Jews gradually stopped using the Hebrew language, especially biblical Hebrew. A translated Bible became a basic necessity for the reading of the Torah in the synagogues, which was performed by two people - one who read the verse is in the original language, and an interpreter repeats his words in the spoken language.

The Bible translations can be divided into two main types - Jewish translations and Christian translations. There are a number of differences between the two, the most prominent of which is the inclusion of the New Testament in Christian translations as opposed to its absence in Jewish translations. The Jewish translations were made mainly from the original Hebrew text, and most of the early Jewish translations were made only into separate parts of the Bible, with the intention that they will be used as a commentary on the Bible. In contrast, the Christian translations are mostly intended for independent use, and most of them are based on the Greek translation translated into Latin - the Latin Vulgate.

The truth is that the Holy Scriptures should not be translated into any language. But because of an act explained in the Talmud there was no choice and the Jews translated it.

**And the story is:**

And this was due to the incident of King Ptolemy, as it is taught in a Baraita: There was an incident involving King Ptolemy of Egypt, who assembled seventy-two Elders from the Sages of Israel, and put them into seventy-two separate rooms, and did not reveal to them for what purpose he assembled them, so that they would not coordinate their responses. He entered and approached each and every one, and said to each of them: Write for me a translation of the Torah of Moses your teacher. The Holy One, Blessed be He, placed wisdom in the heart of each and every one, and they all agreed to one common understanding. Not only did they all translate the text correctly, they all introduced the same changes into the translated text.

And the Talmud [Megillah 9a] continues to say that all 72 sages did not translate it exactly, but changed several verses, for example:

And they wrote for him: God created in the beginning [**Bereshit**], reversing the order of the words in the first phrase in the Torah that could be misinterpreted as: **Bereshit created God** [Genesis 1:1]. Instead of: Come, let us go down, and there confound their language [Genesis 11:7], which indicates multiple authorities, they wrote in the singular: Come, let me go down, and there confound their language. In addition, they replaced the verse: "And Sarah laughed within herself [**bekirba**] [Genesis 18:12], with: And Sarah laughed among her relatives [**bikroveha**].

They made this change to distinguish between Sarah's laughter, which God criticized, and Abraham's laughter, to which no reaction is recorded. Based on the change, Sarah's laughter was offensive because she voiced it to others....

The church father Hieronymus [about 325-420], who knew Hebrew in addition to Latin and Greek, and specialized in theology, created an improved homogenous translation from all the Latin translations. In his work, which was done between the years 390-405, he was greatly assisted by the Jews he knew. The translation of the first books he dealt with [first prophets, Samuel and kings] was done closely to the Hebrew text, but the last books [Joshua, Judges, Ruth and Esther] were translated by him in a freer manner. In any case, Hieronymus relied on the Hebrew version, because he noticed the deviations that the Greek translations have from the Hebrew original.

The Vulgate was recognized by the Church in 1546 as the authoritative text of the Holy Scriptures. It includes, apart from the books of the Bible and the New Testament, also the translation of the external books. The name **Vulgate** [=Common] can be translated by Roger Bacon, and when the internal division into chapters was made in the Vulgate.

The English translation - a translation of parts of the Bible into English was made starting from the 7th century. A complete translation of the Bible into English, made under the direction of John Wycliffe, from the Latin version of the Vulgate, was published in about 1380. The church condemned this translation, because it saw the interpretation that accompanied it as heretical. Further English translations were also rejected by the church and the king.

In 1530 William Tyndale translated only the Pentateuch from the Greek in the Kaspela edition into English, and 5 years later Miles Coverdale published the entire Bible in English. James I, King of England initiated the creation of an official translation of the Bible and the New Testament into English. His initiative came against the background of the bitter struggle between Protestants and Catholics in England and Scotland. King James proposed to write a new English translation that would be acceptable to Protestants and Catholics alike. This translation, made from Hebrew and Greek, was published in 1611, and is called the "King James Version, KJV". This translation is still considered the authorized translation of the English Bible [Authorized Version]; Researchers from the universities of London, Oxford and Cambridge worked on it. They also used a Jewish commentary for the translation. In this edition, King James demanded to cleanse the kings of any evil that could cling to them, in order to purify the institution of the monarchy. In the translation, an effort was made to maintain the structure of the Hebrew text, and to convert as much as possible a Hebrew word into an English word. However, a Hebrew word may be translated into different words in English in different contexts, this is to keep the language fluid. The attempt to literally translate Hebrew idioms created new expressions in English, which gradually became part of the English language and culture.

# The Book of Exodus

The Book of **Names** is the second book in the Torah. It is called so because the second word in the book is "names" - "And these are the names of the children of Israel coming from Egypt, Jacob, Ish, and his house came". In the Greek translations the book is called Exodus (Greek: ὁδός = road, -ἐξ = from) after the great event described in it - the exodus of the people of Israel from Egypt. This name was preserved in translations into Latin and because of this, it was established as his name in the many languages into which it was translated from Latin. In the Great Laws, it is called "The Second Book", and the Ramban calls it "The Book of Exile and Redemption".

The book of Exodus talks about the slavery of the Bnei Israel in Egypt, their exodus from Egypt after the Ten Plagues, and their wanderings in the desert. The description of the wanderings combines various stories and events, culminating in the Torah's giving on Mount Sinai. It also talks about Israel's war with Amalek and the sin of the calf. The book includes many chapters with various commandments, and most of its second part deals with establishing the Mishkan. The central human figure in the book is Moses, the leader of Israel throughout their wanderings in the desert.
At the beginning of the book, there is an associative link with the end of the book of Genesis, by the

number of Israelites coming down from Egypt. Then the scripture talks about the drastic change in the attitude of the Egyptians to the Israelites - from welcome guests they become slaves. Out of the people of the slaves grows a leader named Moses, who grew up in the house of Pharaoh, king of Egypt. The Book of Exodus includes the passages of the Exodus from Egypt, the status of Mount Sinai, the establishment of the "Tabernacle of the Testimonies" and the sin of the calf.

**It should be known that wherever it is written in the Torah <u>"The people"</u> the reference is not to the Israelites themselves but to A mixed multitude that went up with them. As it is written in Exodus 12:38 - Moreover, a mixed multitude went up with them, and very much livestock, both flocks, and herds.**

Moses comes out and sees the Jewish People in slavery. When he notices the Egyptians hitting a Hebrew man - Moses killed him. This became known to Pharaoh and Moses fled to **Midian**, through the Sinai desert, areas where he would lead his people. In **Midian** he helps the daughters of the local priest, Jethro. Moses marries one of his daughters and works as a shepherd. When he went out into the desert, he saw a bush that was burning but not consumed, and from it God revealed himself to him and ordered him to go to Pharaoh and free the Israelites. Moses hesitates and tries to avoid the mission for various reasons. Still, God answers his questions, equips him with signs (supernatural acts) to convince the people, and promises him the cooperation of his older brother Aaron.

Moses and Aaron gather the elders of the people, tell them the word of God, and perform the signs, and the people believe them. They come to Pharaoh and ask him in the name of God to release the people into the desert for three days so that they can celebrate as a nation. Pharaoh refuses and even burdens the Israelites with the burden of work, who blame Moses and Aaron for this. God sends Moses to the people with a promise of liberation from slavery, but the people are tired of work and do not listen to him. Moses is again sent to Pharaoh with a demand to release the people, and even shows him signals, but the king's horns make similar signals, Pharaoh is not impressed and stands by his refusal.

God inflicts a series of severe blows on Egypt: the water of the Nile turns to blood, the land is filled with frogs, lice, and locusts, the diseases of the plague and boils torment the animals and the people, hail and locusts destroy the crops, darkness pervades the land and finally - the firstborns of Egypt are killed.

In all the plagues, the Israelites, who lived in the land of Goshen, hardly suffered. During some of the plagues, Pharaoh relents and agrees to release the Israelites, but after the plague is over, he hardens his heart and returns.

Before the plague of firstborns, which will cause Pharaoh to break and free the people, God instructs the Israelites how to defend themselves against the plague and how to prepare for the exodus from Egypt, and establishes the holiday of Passover, so called because God passed over the houses of Israel and killed only the firstborn of Egypt, the mitzvot of the holiday (such as prohibiting eating chametz) and the mitzvah of redeeming the son, which is also related to the firstborn.

Following the plague of firstborns, Pharaoh surrenders and frees the Israelites, but later he regrets it again and goes after them. They reach the Red Sea which has been divided in two allowing them to cross it by land inside the sea.

The Egyptians chase them into the passage, but the sea closes in on them and they drown. After the miracle, the Israelites burst into a song known as the - **Song of the Sea**.

As soon as they entered the Sinai desert, the Israelites complained about the lack of water. This event opens a tract of repeated stories about the people's fear of trusting Moses and God's providence, which requires God's miraculous intervention - and Moses as a mediator.

When the Israelites arrive at **Rapidim**, the people are thirsty again and Moses strikes the rock and makes it release water.

In the continuation of the wanderings, the people of Israel are attacked by a tribe of nomads named **Amalek**, but Israel defeats them.

The Israelites arrive at Mount Sinai and there they receive the Torah - a branched set of laws and commandments, chief among them the Ten Commandments spoken to the people by God himself.

The people are afraid of the noise and the smoke rising from the mountain, and they ask Moses to stay alone with God and speak to them in his name.

Moses calms the people, who have retreated from the mountain and come to hear from God the laws of the Torah, which are detailed later.

Moses hands over to the Israelites the set of Torah mitzvahs that they must observe. These commandments include, among other things, laws of slavery, honoring parents, laws of theft, damages, protecting the weak, legal laws, Shamita, and more.

Moses lingers on the mountain for many days, until the people's patience runs out and they ask Aaron to make them a god who will go before them in the desert. Aaron collects the gold jewelry of the people and melts it down, and the people make a statue of a calf from the gold.

# Exodus

## Shemot

## Chapter 1

**1.** Now these are the names of the sons of Israel, who came into Egypt with Jacob; every man came with his household:

**2.** Reuben, Simeon, Levi, and Judah;

**3.** Issachar, Zebulun, and Benjamin;

**4.** Dan and Naphtali, Gad and Asher.

**5.** And all the souls that came out of the loins of Jacob were seventy souls; and Joseph was in Egypt already.

**6.** And Joseph died, and all his brethren, and all that generation.

**7.** And the children of Israel were fruitful, and increased abundantly, and multiplied, and waxed exceeding mighty; and the land was filled with them.

**8.** Now there arose a new king over Egypt, who knew not Joseph.

**9.** And he said unto his people: Behold, the people of the children of Israel are too many and too mighty for us;

**10.** Come, let us deal wisely with them, lest they multiply, and it come to pass, that, when there befalleth us any war, they also join themselves unto our enemies, and fight against us, and get them up out of the land.

**11.** Therefore, they did set over them taskmasters to afflict them with their burdens. And they built for Pharaoh store-cities, Pithom and Raamses.

**12.** But the more they afflicted them, the more they multiplied and the more they spread abroad. And they were adread because of the children of Israel.

**13.** And the Egyptians made the children of Israel to serve with rigour.

**14.** And they made their lives bitter with hard service, in mortar and in brick, and in all manner of service in the field; in all their service, wherein they made them serve with rigour.

**15.** And the king of Egypt spoke to the Hebrew midwives, of whom the name of the one was Shiphrah, and the name of the other Puah;

**16.** And he said: When ye do the office of a midwife to the Hebrew women, ye shall look upon the birthstool: if it be a son, then ye shall kill him; but if it be a daughter, then she shall live.

**17.** But the midwives feared God, and did not as the king of Egypt commanded them, but saved the men-children alive.

**18.** And the king of Egypt called for the midwives, and said unto them: Why have ye done this thing, and have saved the men-children alive?

**19.** And the midwives said unto Pharaoh: Because the Hebrew women are not as the Egyptian women; for they are lively, and are delivered ere the midwife come unto them.

**20.** And God dealt well with the midwives; and the people multiplied, and waxed very mighty.

**21.** And it came to pass, because the midwives feared God, that He made them houses.

**22.** And Pharaoh charged all his people, saying: Every son that is born ye shall cast into the river, and every daughter ye shall save alive.

## Chapter 2

**1.** And there went a man of the house of Levi, and took to wife a daughter of Levi.

**2.** And the woman conceived, and bore a son; and when she saw him that he was a goodly child, she hid him three months.

**3.** And when she could not longer hide him, she took for him an ark of bulrushes, and daubed it with slime and with pitch; and she put the child therein, and laid it in the flags by the river's brink.

**4.** And his sister stood afar off, to know what would be done to him.

**5.** And the daughter of Pharaoh came down to bathe in the river; and her maidens walked along by the river-side; and she saw the ark among the flags, and sent her handmaid to fetch it.

**6.** And she opened it, and saw it, even the child; and behold a boy that wept. And she had compassion on him, and said: This is one of the **Hebrews children**.

**7.** Then  said his sister to Pharaoh's daughter: Shall I

go and call thee a nurse of the Hebrew women, that she may nurse the child for thee?

**8.** And Pharaoh's daughter said to her: Go. And the maiden went and called the child's mother.

**9.** And Pharaoh's daughter said unto her: Take this child away, and nurse it for me, and I will give thee thy wages. And the woman took the child, and nursed it.

**10.** And the child grew, and she brought him unto Pharaoh's daughter, and he became her son. And she called his name Moses, and said: Because I drew him out of the water.

**11.** And it came to pass in those days, when Moses was grown up, that he went out unto his brethren, and looked on their burdens; and he saw an Egyptian smiting a Hebrew, one of his brethren.

**12.** And he looked this way and that way, and when he saw that there was no man, he smote the Egyptian, and hid him in the sand.

**13.** And he went out the second day, and, behold, two men of the Hebrews were striving together; and he said to him that did the wrong: Wherefore smitest thou, thy fellow?

**14.** And he said: Who made thee a ruler and a judge over us? thinkest thou to kill me, as thou didst kill the Egyptian? And Moses feared, and said: Surely the thing is known.

**15.** Now when Pharaoh heard this thing, he sought to slay Moses. But Moses fled from the face of Pharaoh, and dwelt in the land of Midian; and he sat down by a well.

**16.** Now the priest of Midian had seven daughters; and they came and drew water, and filled the troughs to water their father's flock.

**17.** And the shepherds came and drove them away; but Moses stood up and helped them, and watered their flock.

**18.** And when they came to **Reuel** their father, he said: How is it that ye are come so soon to-day?

**19.** And they said: An Egyptian delivered us out of the hand of the shepherds, and moreover he drew water for us, and watered the flock.

**20.** And he said unto his daughters: And where is he? Why is it that ye have left the man? call him, that he may eat bread.

**21.** And Moses was content to dwell with the man; and he gave Moses Zipporah his daughter.

**22.** And she bore a son, and he called his name Gershom; for he said: I have been a stranger in a strange land.

**23.** And it came to pass in the course of those many days that the king of Egypt died; and the children of Israel sighed by reason of the bondage, and they cried, and their cry came up unto God by reason of the bondage.

**24.** And God heard their groaning, and God remembered His covenant with Abraham, with Isaac, and with Jacob.

**25.** And God saw the children of Israel, and God took cognizance of them.

## Chapter 3

**1.** Now Moses was keeping the flock of Jethro his father-in-law, the priest of Midian; and he led the flock to the farthest end of the wilderness, and came to the mountain of God, unto Horeb.

**2.** And the angel of the LORD appeared unto him in a flame of fire out of the midst of a bush; and he looked, and, behold, the bush burned with fire, and the bush was not consumed.

**3.** And Moses said: I will turn aside now, and see this great sight, why the bush is not burnt.

**4.** And when the LORD saw that he turned aside to see, God called unto him out of the midst of the bush, and said: **Moses Moses**. And he said: Here am I.

**5.** And He said: Draw not nigh hither; put off thy shoes from off thy feet, for the place whereon thou standest is holy ground.

**6.** Moreover, He said: I am the God of thy father, the God of Abraham, the God of Isaac, and the God of Jacob. And Moses hid his face; for he was afraid to look upon God.

**7.** And the LORD said: I have surely seen the affliction of My people that are in Egypt, and have heard their cry by reason of their taskmasters; for I know their pains;

**8.** And  I am  come down  to deliver them out of the

hand of the Egyptians, and to bring them up out of that land unto a good land and a large, unto a land flowing with milk and honey; unto the place of the Canaanite, and the Hittite, and the Amorite, and the Perizzite, and the Hivite, and the Jebusite.

**9.** And now, behold, the cry of the children of Israel is come unto Me; moreover, I have seen the oppression wherewith the Egyptians oppress them.

**10.** Come now therefore, and I will send thee unto Pharaoh, that thou mayest bring forth My people the children of Israel out of Egypt.

**11.** And Moses said unto God: Who am I, that I should go unto Pharaoh, and that I should bring forth the children of Israel out of Egypt?

**12.** And He said: Certainly, I will be with thee; and this shall be the token unto thee, that I have sent thee: when thou hast brought forth the people out of Egypt, ye shall serve God upon this mountain.

**13.** And Moses said unto God: Behold, when I come unto the children of Israel, and shall say unto them: The God of your fathers hath sent me unto you; and they shall say to me: What is His name? what shall I say unto them?

**14.** And God said unto Moses: **Ehyeh-Asher-Ehyeh** [I am that I am]; and He said: Thus, shalt thou say unto the children of Israel: I AM hath sent me unto you.

**15.** And God said moreover unto Moses: Thus, shalt thou say unto the children of Israel: The LORD, the

God of your fathers, the God of Abraham, the God of Isaac, and the God of Jacob, hath sent me unto you; this is My name for ever, and this is My memorial unto all generations.

**16.** Go, and gather the elders of Israel together, and say unto them: The LORD, the God of your fathers, the God of Abraham, of Isaac, and of Jacob, hath appeared unto me, saying: I have surely remembered you, and seen that which is done to you in Egypt.

**17.** And I have said: I will bring you up out of the affliction of Egypt unto the land of the Canaanite, and the Hittite, and the Amorite, and the Perizzite, and the Hivite, and the Jebusite, unto a land flowing with milk and honey.

**18.** And they shall hearken to thy voice. And thou shalt come, thou and the elders of Israel, unto the king of Egypt, and ye shall say unto him: The LORD, the God of the Hebrews, hath met with us. And now let us go, we pray thee, three days - journey into the wilderness, that we may sacrifice to the LORD our God.

**19.** And I know that the king of Egypt will not give you leave to go, except by a mighty hand.

**20.** And I will put forth My hand, and smite Egypt with all My wonders which I will do in the midst thereof. And after that he will let you go.

**21.** And I will give this people favour in the sight of the Egyptians. And it shall come to pass, that, when ye go, ye shall not go empty;

**22.** But every woman shall ask of her neighbour, and of her that sojourneth in her house, jewels of silver, and jewels of gold, and raiment; and ye shall put them upon your sons, and upon your daughters; and ye shall spoil the Egyptians.

## Chapter 4

**1.** And Moses answered and said: But, behold, they will not believe me, nor hearken unto my voice; for they will say: The lord hath not appeared unto thee.

**2.** And the LORD said unto him: What is that in thy hand? And he said: A rod.

**3.** And He said: Cast it on the ground. And he cast it on the ground, and it became a serpent; and Moses fled from before it.

**4.** And the LORD said unto Moses: Put forth thy hand, and take it by the tail and he put forth his hand, and laid hold of it, and it became a rod in his hand,

**5.** That they may believe that the LORD, the God of their fathers, the God of Abraham, the God of Isaac, and the God of Jacob, hath appeared unto thee.

**6.** And the LORD said furthermore unto him: Put now thy hand into thy bosom. And he put his hand into his bosom; and when he took it out, behold, his hand was leprous, as white as snow.

**7.** And He said: Put thy hand back into thy bosom. And he put his hand back into his bosom; and when he took it out of his bosom, behold, it was turned again as his other flesh.

**8.** And it shall come to pass, if they will not believe thee, neither hearken to the voice of the first sign, that they will believe the voice of the latter sign.

**9.** And it shall come to pass, if they will not believe even these two signs, neither hearken unto thy voice, that thou shalt take of the water of the river, and pour it upon the dry land; and the water which thou takest out of the river shall become blood upon the dry land.

**10.** And Moses said unto the LORD: Oh Lord, I am not a man of words, neither heretofore, nor since Thou hast spoken unto Thy servant; for I am slow of speech, and of a slow tongue.

**11.** And the LORD said unto him: Who hath made man's mouth? or who maketh a man dumb, or deaf, or seeing, or blind? is it not I the LORD?

**12.** Now therefore go, and I will be with thy mouth, and teach thee what thou shalt speak.

**13.** And he said: Oh Lord, send, I pray Thee, by the hand of him whom Thou wilt send.

**14.** And the anger of the LORD was kindled against Moses, and He said: Is there not Aaron thy brother the Levite? I know that he can speak well. And also, behold, he cometh forth to meet thee; and when he seeth thee, he will be glad in his heart.

**15.** And thou shalt speak unto him, and put the words in his mouth; and I will be with thy mouth, and with his mouth, and will teach you what ye shall do.

**16.** And he shall be thy spokesman unto the people; and it shall come to pass, that he shall be to the a mouth, and thou shalt be to him in God's stead.

**17.** And thou shalt take in thy hand this rod, wherewith thou shalt do the signs.

**18.** And Moses went and returned to Jethro his father-in-law, and said unto him: Let me go, I pray thee, and unto my brethren that are in Egypt, and see whether they be yet alive. And Jethro said to Moses: Go in peace.

**19.** And the LORD said unto Moses in Midian: Go, return into Egypt; for all the men are dead that sought thy life.

**20.** And Moses took his wife and his sons, and set them upon an ass, and he returned to the land of Egypt; and Moses took the rod of God in his hand.

**21.** And the LORD said unto Moses: When thou goest back into Egypt, see that thou do before Pharaoh all the wonders which I have put in thy hand; but I will harden his heart, and he will not let the people go.

**22.** And thou shalt say unto Pharaoh: Thus, saith the LORD: Israel is My son, My first-born.

**23.** And I have said unto thee: Let My son Go, that he may serve Me; and thou hast refused to let him go. Behold, I will slay thy first-born.

**24.** And it came to pass on the way at the lodging-place, that the LORD met him, and sought to kill him.

**25.** Then Zipporah took a flint, and cut off the foreskin of her son, and cast it at his feet; and she said: Surely a bridegroom of blood art thou to me.

**26.** So, he let him alone. Then she said: A bridegroom

of blood in regard of the circumcision.

**27.** And the LORD said to Aaron: Go into the wilderness to meet Moses. And he went, and met him in the mountain of God, and kissed him.

**28.** And Moses told Aaron all the words of the LORD wherewith He had sent him, and all the signs wherewith He had charged him.

**29.** And Moses and Aaron went and gathered together all the elders of the children of Israel.

**30.** And Aaron spoke all the words which the LORD had spoken unto Moses, and did the signs in the sight of the people.

**31.** And the people believed; and when they heard that the LORD had remembered the children of Israel, and that He had seen their affliction, then they bowed their heads and worshipped.

## Chapter 5

**1.** And afterward Moses and Aaron came, and said unto Pharaoh: Thus, saith the LORD, the God of Israel: Let My people go, that they may hold a feast unto Me in the wilderness.

**2.** And Pharaoh said: Who is the LORD, that I should hearken unto His voice to let Israel go? I know not the LORD, and moreover I will not let Israel go.

**3.** And they said: The God of the Hebrews hath met with us. Let us go, we pray thee, three days - journey into the wilderness, and sacrifice unto the LORD our God; lest He fall upon us with pestilence, or with the sword.

**4.** And the king of Egypt said unto them: Wherefore do ye, Moses and Aaron, cause the people to break loose from their work? get you unto your burdens.

**5.** And Pharaoh said: Behold, the people of the land are now many, and will ye make them rest from their burdens?

**6.** And the same day Pharaoh commanded the taskmasters of the people, and their officers, saying:

**7.** Ye shall no more give the people straw to make brick, as heretofore. Let them go and gather straw for themselves.

**8.** And the tale of the bricks, which they did make heretofore, ye shall lay upon them; ye shall not diminish aught thereof; for they are idle; therefore, they cry, saying: Let us go and sacrifice to our God.

**9.** Let heavier work be laid upon the men, that they may labour therein; and let them not regard lying words.

**10.** And the taskmasters of the people went out, and their officers, and they spoke to the people, saying: Thus, saith Pharaoh: I will not give you straw.

**11.** Go yourselves, get you straw where ye can find it; for nought of your work shall be diminished.

**12.** So, the people were scattered abroad throughout all the land of Egypt to gather stubble for straw.

**13.** And the taskmasters were urgent, saying: Fulfil your work, your daily task, as when there was straw.

**14.** And  the officers  of the  children of Israel, whom

Pharaoh's taskmasters had set over them, were beaten, saying: Wherefore have ye not fulfilled your appointed task in making brick both yesterday and today as heretofore?

**15.** Then the officers of the children of Israel came and cried unto Pharaoh, saying: Wherefore dealest thou thus with thy servants?

**16.** There is no straw given unto thy servants, and they say to us: Make brick; and, behold, thy servants are beaten, but the fault is in thine own people.

**17.** But he said: Ye are idle, ye are idle; therefore, ye say: Let us go and sacrifice to the LORD.

**18.** Go therefore now, and work; for there shall no straw be given you, yet shall ye deliver the tale of bricks.

**19.** And the officers of the children of Israel did see that they were set on mischief, when they said: Ye shall not diminish aught from your bricks, your daily task.

**20.** And they met Moses and Aaron, who stood in the way, as they came forth from Pharaoh;

**21.** And they said unto them: The LORD look upon you, and judge; because ye have made our savour to be abhorred in the eyes of Pharaoh, and in the eyes of his servants, to put a sword in their hand to slay us.

**22.** And Moses returned unto the LORD, and said: Lord, wherefore hast Thou dealt ill with this people? why is it that Thou hast sent me?

**23.** For since I came to Pharaoh to speak in Thy name,

he hath dealt ill with this people; neither hast Thou delivered Thy people at all.

## Chapter 6

**1.** And the LORD said unto Moses: Now shalt thou see what I will do to Pharaoh; for by a strong hand shall he let them go, and by a strong hand shall he drive them out of his land.

## Vaera

**2.** And God spoke unto Moses, and said unto him: I am the LORD;

**3.** And I appeared unto Abraham, unto Isaac, and unto Jacob, as God Almighty, but by My name יהוה I made Me not known to them.

**4.** And I have also established My covenant with them, to give them the land of Canaan, the land of their sojournings, wherein they sojourned.

**5.** And moreover, I have heard the groaning of the children of Israel, whom the Egyptians keep in bondage; and I have remembered My covenant.

**6.** Wherefore say unto the children of Israel: I am the LORD, and I will bring you out from under the burdens of the Egyptians, and I will deliver you from their bondage, and I will redeem you with an outstretched arm, and with great judgments;

**7.** And I will take you to Me for a people, and I will be to you a God; and ye shall know that I am the

LORD your God, who brought you out from under the burdens of the Egyptians.

**8.** And I will bring you in unto the land, concerning which I lifted up My hand to give it to Abraham, to Isaac, and to Jacob; and I will give it you for a heritage: I am the LORD.

**9.** And Moses spoke so unto the children of Israel; but they hearkened not unto Moses for impatience of spirit, and for cruel bondage.

**10.** And the LORD spoke unto Moses, saying:

**11.** Go in, speak unto Pharaoh king of Egypt, that he let the children of Israel go out of his land.

**12.** And Moses spoke before the LORD, saying: Behold, the children of Israel have not hearkened unto me; how then shall Pharaoh hear me, who am of uncircumcised lips?

**13.** And the LORD spoke unto Moses and unto Aaron, and gave them a charge unto the children of Israel, and unto Pharaoh king of Egypt, to bring the children of Israel out of the land of Egypt.

**14.** These are the heads of their fathers' houses: the sons of Reuben the first-born of Israel: Hanoch, and Pallu, Hezron, and Carmi. These are the families of Reuben.

**15.** And the sons of Simeon: Jemuel, and Jamin, and Ohad, and Jachin, and Zohar, and Shaul the son of a Canaanitish woman. These are the families of Simeon.

**16.** And these are the names of the sons of Levi

according to their generations: Gershon and Kohath, and Merari. And the years of the life of Levi were a hundred thirty and seven years.

**17.** The sons of Gershon: Libni and Shimei, according to their families.

**18.** And the sons of Kohath: Amram, and Izhar, and Hebron, and Uzziel. And the years of the life of Kohath were a hundred thirty and three years.

**19.** And the sons of Merari: Mahli and Mushi. These are the families of the Levites according to their generations.

**20.** And Amram took him Jochebed his father's sister to wife; and she bore him Aaron and Moses. And the years of the life of Amram were a hundred and thirty and seven years.

**21.** And the sons of Izhar: Korah, and Nepheg, and Zichri.

**22.** And the sons of Uzziel: Mishael, and Elzaphan, and Sithri.

**23.** And Aaron took him Elisheba, the daughter of Amminadab, the sister of Nahshon, to wife; and she bore him Nadab and Abihu, Eleazar and Ithamar.

**24.** And the sons of Korah: Assir, and Elkanah, and Abiasaph; these are the families of the Korahites.

**25.** And Eleazar Aaron's son took him one of the daughters of Putiel to wife; and she bore him Phinehas. These are the heads of the fathers' houses of the Levites according to their families.

**26.** These are that Aaron and Moses, to whom the

LORD said: Bring out the children of Israel from the land of Egypt according to their hosts.

**27.** These are they that spoke to Pharaoh king of Egypt, to bring out the children of Israel from Egypt. These are that Moses and Aaron.

**28.** And it came to pass on the day when the LORD spoke unto Moses in the land of Egypt,

**29.** That the LORD spoke unto Moses, saying: I am the LORD; speak thou unto Pharaoh king of Egypt all that I speak unto thee.

**30.** And Moses said before the LORD: Behold, I am of uncircumcised lips, and how shall Pharaoh hearken unto me?

## Chapter 7

**1.** And the LORD said unto Moses: See, I have set thee in God's stead to Pharaoh; and Aaron thy brother shall be thy prophet.

**2.** Thou shalt speak all that I command thee; and Aaron thy brother shall speak unto Pharaoh, that he let the children of Israel go out of his land.

**3.** And I will harden Pharaoh's heart, and multiply My signs and My wonders in the land of Egypt.

**4.** But Pharaoh will not hearken unto you, and I will lay My hand upon Egypt, and bring forth My hosts, My people the children of Israel, out of the land of Egypt, by great judgments.

**5.** And the Egyptians shall know that I am the LORD, when I stretch forth My hand upon  Egypt, and  bring out the children of Israel from among them.

**6.** And Moses and Aaron did so; as the LORD commanded them, so did they.

**7.** And Moses was fourscore years old, and Aaron fourscore and three years old, when they spoke unto Pharaoh.

**8.** And the LORD spoke unto Moses and unto Aaron, saying:

**9.** When Pharaoh shall speak unto you, saying: Show a wonder for you; then thou shalt say unto Aaron: Take thy rod, and cast it down before Pharaoh, that it become a serpent.

**10.** And Moses and Aaron went in unto Pharaoh, and they did so, as the LORD had commanded; and Aaron cast down his rod before Pharaoh and before his servants, and it became a serpent.

**11.** Then Pharaoh also called for the wise men and the sorcerers; and they also, the magicians of Egypt, did in like manner with their secret arts.

**12.** For they cast down every man his rod, and they became serpents; but Aaron's rod swallowed up their rods.

**13.** And Pharaoh's heart was hardened, and he hearkened not unto them; as the LORD had spoken.

**14.** And the LORD said unto Moses: Pharaoh's heart is stubborn, he refuseth to let the people go.

**15.** Get thee unto Pharaoh in the morning; lo, he goeth out unto the water; and thou shalt stand by the river's brink to meet him; and the rod which was turned to a serpent shalt thou take in thy hand.

**16.** And thou shalt say unto him: The LORD, the God of the Hebrews, hath sent me unto thee, saying: Let My people go, that they may serve Me in the wilderness; and, behold, hitherto thou hast not hearkened;

**17.** Thus, saith the LORD: In this thou shalt know that I am the LORD behold, I will smite with the rod that is in my hand upon the waters which are in the river, and they shall be turned to blood.

**18.** And the fish that are in the river shall die, and the river shall become foul; and the Egyptians shall loathe to drink water from the river.

**19.** And the LORD said unto Moses: Say unto Aaron: Take thy rod, and stretch out thy hand over the waters of Egypt, over their rivers, over their streams, and over their pools, and over all their ponds of water, that they may become blood; and there shall be blood throughout all the land of Egypt, both in vessels of wood and in vessels of stone.

**20.** And Moses and Aaron did so, as the LORD commanded; and he lifted up the rod, and smote the waters that were in the river, in the sight of Pharaoh, and in the sight of his servants; and all the waters that were in the river were turned to blood.

**21.** And the fish that were in the river died; and the river became foul, and the Egyptians could not drink water from the river; and the blood was throughout all the land of Egypt.

**22.** And the magicians of Egypt did in like manner with their secret arts; and Pharaoh's heart was hardened, and he hearkened not unto them; as the LORD had spoken.

**23.** And Pharaoh turned and went into his house, neither did he lay even this to heart.

**24.** And all the Egyptians digged round about the river for water to drink; for they could not drink of the water of the river.

**25.** And seven days were fulfilled, after that the LORD had smitten the river.

**26.** And the LORD spoke unto Moses: Go in unto Pharaoh, and say unto him: Thus, saith the LORD: Let My people go, that they may serve Me.

**27.** And if thou refuse to let them go, behold, I will smite all thy borders with frogs.

**28.** And the river shall swarm with frogs, which shall go up and come into thy house, and into thy bed-chamber, and upon thy bed, and into the house of thy servants, and upon thy people, and into thine ovens, and into thy kneading-troughs.

**29.** And the frogs shall come up both upon thee, and upon thy people, and upon all thy servants.


## Chapter 8

**1.** And the LORD said unto Moses: Say unto Aaron: Stretch forth thy hand with thy rod over the rivers, over the canals, and over the pools, and cause frogs to come up upon the land of Egypt.

**2.** And Aaron stretched out his hand over the waters of Egypt; and the frogs came up, and covered the land of Egypt.

**3.** And the magicians did in like manner with their secret arts, and brought up frogs upon the land of Egypt.

**4.** Then Pharaoh called for Moses and Aaron, and said: Entreat the LORD, that He take away the frogs from me, and from my people; and I will let the people go, that they may sacrifice unto the LORD.

**5.** And Moses said unto Pharaoh: Have thou this glory over me; against what time shall I entreat for thee, and for thy servants, and for thy people, that the frogs be destroyed from thee and thy houses, and remain in the river only?

**6.** And he said: Against to-morrow. And he said: Be it according to thy word; that thou mayest know that there is none like unto the LORD our God.

**7.** And the frogs shall depart from thee, and from thy houses, and from thy servants, and from thy people; they shall remain in the river only.

**8.** And Moses and Aaron went out from Pharaoh; and Moses cried unto the LORD concerning the frogs, which He had brought upon Pharaoh.

**9.** And the LORD did according to the word of Moses; and the frogs died out of the houses, out of the courts, and out of the fields.

**10.** And they gathered them together in heaps; and the land stank.

**11.** But when Pharaoh saw that there was respite, he hardened his heart, and hearkened not unto them; as the LORD had spoken.

**12.** And the LORD said unto Moses: Say unto Aaron: Stretch out thy rod, and smite the dust of the earth, that it may become gnats throughout all the land of Egypt.

**13.** And they did so; and Aaron stretched out his hand with his rod, and smote the dust of the earth, and there were gnats upon man, and upon beast; all the dust of the earth became gnats throughout all the land of Egypt.

**14.** And the magicians did so with their secret arts to bring forth gnats, but they could not; and there were gnats upon man, and upon beast.

**15.** Then the magicians said unto Pharaoh: This is the finger of God; and Pharaoh's heart was hardened, and he hearkened not unto them; as the LORD had spoken.

**16.** And the LORD said unto Moses: Rise up early in the morning, and stand before Pharaoh; lo, he cometh forth to the water; and say unto him: Thus, saith the LORD: Let My people go, that they may serve Me.

**17.** Else, if thou wilt not let My people go, behold, I will send swarms of flies upon thee, and upon thy servants, and upon thy people, and into thy houses; and the houses of the Egyptians shall be full of swarms of flies, and also the ground whereon they are.

**18.** And I will set apart in that day the land of Goshen, in which My people dwell, that no swarms of flies shall be there; to the end that thou mayest know that I am the LORD in the midst of the earth.

**19.** And I will put a division between My people and thy people-by to-morrow shall this sign be.

**20.** And the LORD did so; and there came grievous swarms of flies into the house of Pharaoh, and into his servants' houses; and in all the land of Egypt the land was ruined by reason of the swarms of flies.

**21.** And Pharaoh called for Moses and for Aaron, and said: Go ye, sacrifice to your God in the land.

**22.** And Moses said: It is not meet so to do; for we shall sacrifice the abomination of the Egyptians to the LORD our God; lo, if we sacrifice the abomination of the Egyptians before their eyes, will they not stone us?

**23.** We will go three days - journey into the wilderness, and sacrifice to the LORD our God, as He shall command us.

**24.** And Pharaoh said: I will let you go, that ye may sacrifice to the LORD your God in the wilderness; only ye shall not go very far away; entreat for me.

**25.** And Moses said: Behold, I go out from thee, and I will entreat the LORD that the swarms of flies may depart from Pharaoh, from his servants, and from his people, tomorrow; only let not Pharaoh deal deceitfully any more in not letting the people go to sacrifice to the LORD.

**26.** And Moses went out from Pharaoh, and entreated the LORD.

**27.** And the LORD did according to the word of Moses; and He removed the swarms of flies from Pharaoh, from his servants, and from his people; there remained not one.

**28.** And Pharaoh hardened his heart this time also, and he did not let the people go.

## Chapter 9

**1.** Then the LORD said unto Moses: Go in unto Pharaoh, and tell him: Thus, saith the LORD, the God of the Hebrews: Let My people go, that they may serve Me.

**2.** For if thou refuse to let them go, and wilt hold them still,

**3.** Behold, the hand of the LORD is upon thy cattle which are in the field, upon the horses, upon the asses, upon the camels, upon the herds, and upon the flocks; there shall be a very grievous murrain.

**4.** And the LORD shall make a division between the cattle of Israel and the cattle of Egypt; and there shall nothing die of all that belongeth to the children of Israel.

**5.** And the LORD appointed a set time, saying: Tomorrow the LORD shall do this thing in the land.

**6.** And the LORD did that thing on the morrow, and all the cattle of Egypt died; but of the cattle of the children of Israel died not one.

**7.** And Pharaoh sent, and, behold, there was not so much as one of the cattle of the Israelites dead. But the heart of Pharaoh was stubborn, and he did not let the people go.

**8.** And the LORD said unto Moses and unto Aaron: Take to you handfuls of soot of the furnace, and let Moses throw it heavenward in the sight of Pharaoh.

**9.** And it shall become small dust over all the land of Egypt, and shall be a boil breaking forth with blains upon man and upon beast, throughout all the land of Egypt.

**10.** And they took soot of the furnace, and stood before Pharaoh; and Moses threw it up heavenward; and it became a boil breaking forth with blains upon man and upon beast.

**11.** And the magicians could not stand before Moses because of the boils; for the boils were upon the magicians, and upon all the Egyptians.

**12.** And the LORD hardened the heart of Pharaoh, and he hearkened not unto them; as the LORD had spoken unto Moses.

**13.** And the LORD said unto Moses: Rise up early in the morning, and stand before Pharaoh, and say unto him: Thus, saith the LORD, the God of the Hebrews: Let My people go, that they may serve Me.

**14.** For I will this time send all My plagues upon thy person, and upon thy servants, and upon thy people; that thou mayest know that there is none like Me in all the earth.

**15.** Surely now I had put forth My hand, and smitten thee and thy people with pestilence, and thou hadst been cut off from the earth.

**16.** But in very deed for this cause have I made thee to stand, to show thee My power, and that My name may be declared throughout all the earth.

**17.** As yet exaltest thou thyself against My people, that thou wilt not let them go?

**18.** Behold, tomorrow about this time I will cause it to rain a very grievous hail, such as hath not been in Egypt since the day it was founded even until now.

**19.** Now therefore send, hasten in thy cattle and all that thou hast in the field; for every man and beast that shall be found in the field, and shall not be brought home, the hail shall come down upon them, and they shall die.

**20.** He that feared the word of the LORD among the servants of Pharaoh made his servants and his cattle flee into the houses;

**21.** And he that regarded not the word of the LORD left his servants and his cattle in the field.

**22.** And the LORD said unto Moses: Stretch forth thy hand toward heaven, that there may be hail in all the land of Egypt, upon man, and upon beast, and upon every herb of the field, throughout the land of Egypt.

**23.** And Moses stretched forth his rod toward heaven; and the LORD sent thunder and hail, and fire ran down unto the earth; and the LORD caused to hail upon the land of Egypt.

**24.** So, there was hail, and fire flashing up amidst the hail, very grievous, such as had not been in all the land of Egypt since it became a nation.

**25.** And the hail smote throughout all the land of Egypt all that was in the field, both man and beast; and the hail smote every herb of the field, and broke every tree of the field.

**26.** Only in the land of Goshen, where the children of Israel were, was there no hail.

**27.** And Pharaoh sent, and called for Moses and Aaron, and said unto them: I have sinned this time; the LORD is righteous, and I and my people are wicked.

**28.** Entreat the LORD, and let there be enough of these mighty thunderings and hail; and I will let you go, and ye shall stay no longer.

**29.** And Moses said unto him: As soon as I am gone out of the city, I will spread forth my hands unto the LORD; the thunders shall cease, neither shall there be any more hail; that thou mayest know that the earth is the LORD's.

**30.** But as for thee and thy servants, I know that ye will not yet fear the LORD God.

**31.** And the flax and the barley were smitten; for the barley was in the ear, and the flax was in bloom.

**32.** But the wheat and the spelt were not smitten; for they ripen late.

**33.** And Moses went out of the city from Pharaoh, and spread forth his hands unto the LORD; and the thunders and hail ceased, and the rain was not poured upon the earth.

**34.** And when Pharaoh saw that the rain and the hail and the thunders were ceased, he sinned yet more, and hardened his heart, he and his servants.

**35.** And the heart of Pharaoh was hardened, and he did not let the children of Israel go; as the LORD had spoken by Moses.

## Bo

## Chapter 10

**1.** And the LORD said unto Moses: Go in unto Pharaoh; for I have hardened his heart, and the heart of his servants, that I might show these My signs in the midst of them;

**2.** And that thou mayest tell in the ears of thy son, and of thy son's son, what I have wrought upon Egypt, and My signs which I have done among them; that ye may know that I am the LORD.

**3.** And Moses and Aaron went in unto Pharaoh, and said unto him: Thus, saith the LORD, the God of the Hebrews: How long wilt thou refuse to humble thyself before Me? let My people go, that they may serve Me.

**4.** Else, if thou refuse to let My people go, behold, to-morrow will I bring locusts into thy border;

**5.** And they shall cover the face of the earth, that one shall not be able to see the earth; and they shall eat the residue of that which is escaped, which remaineth unto you from the hail, and shall eat every tree which groweth for you out of the field;

**6.** And thy houses shall be filled, and the houses of all thy servants, and the houses of all the Egyptians; as neither thy fathers nor thy fathers - fathers have seen, since the day that they were upon the earth unto this day. And he turned, and went out from Pharaoh.

**7.** And Pharaoh's servants said unto him: How long shall this man be a snare unto us? let the men go, that they may serve the LORD their God, knowest thou not yet that Egypt is destroyed?

**8.** And Moses and Aaron were brought again unto Pharaoh; and he said unto them: Go, serve the LORD your God; but who are they that shall go?

**9.** And Moses said: We will go with our young and with our old, with our sons and with our daughters, with our flocks and with our herds we will go; for we must hold a feast unto the LORD.

**10.** And he said unto them: So be the LORD with you, as I will let you go, and your little ones; see ye that evil is before your face.

**11.** Not so; go now ye that are men, and serve the LORD; for that is what ye desire. And they were driven out from Pharaoh's presence.

**12.** And the LORD said unto Moses: Stretch out thy hand over the land of Egypt for the locusts, that they may come up upon the land of Egypt, and eat every herb of the land, even all that the hail hath left.

**13.** And Moses stretched forth his rod over the land of Egypt, and the LORD brought an east wind upon the land all that day, and all the night; and when it was morning, the east wind brought the locusts.

**14.** And the locusts went up over all the land of Egypt, and rested in all the borders of Egypt; very grievous were they; before them there were no such locusts as they, neither after them shall be such.

**15.** For they covered the face of the whole earth, so that the land was darkened; and they did eat every herb of the land, and all the fruit of the trees which the hail had left; and there remained not any green thing, either tree or herb of the field, through all the land of Egypt.

**16.** Then Pharaoh called for Moses and Aaron in haste; and he said: I have sinned against the LORD your God, and against you.

**17.** Now therefore forgive, I pray thee, my sin only this once, and entreat the LORD your God, that He may take away from me this death only.

**18.** And he went out from Pharaoh, and entreated the LORD.

**19.** And the LORD turned an exceeding strong west wind, which took up the locusts, and drove them into the Red Sea; there remained not one locust in all the border of Egypt.

**20.** But the LORD hardened Pharaoh's heart, and he did not let the children of Israel go.

**21.** And the LORD said  unto Moses: Stretch  out thy

hand toward heaven, that there may be darkness over the land of Egypt, even darkness which may be felt.

**22.** And Moses stretched forth his hand toward heaven; and there was a thick darkness in all the land of Egypt three days;

**23.** They saw not one another, neither rose any from his place for three days; but all the children of Israel had light in their dwellings.

**24.** And Pharaoh called unto Moses, and said: Go ye, serve the LORD; only let your flocks and your herds be stayed; let your little ones also go with you.

**25.** And Moses said: Thou must also give into our hand sacrifices and burnt-offerings, that we may sacrifice unto the LORD our God.

**26.** Our cattle also shall go with us; there shall not a hoof be left behind; for thereof must we take to serve the LORD our God; and we know not with what we must serve the LORD, until we come thither.

**27.** But the LORD hardened Pharaoh's heart, and he would not let them go.

**28.** And Pharaoh said unto him: Get thee from me, take heed to thyself, see my face no more; for in the day, thou seest my face thou shalt die.

**29.** And Moses said: Thou hast spoken well; I will see thy face again no more.


## Chapter 11

**1.** And the LORD said unto Moses: Yet one plague more will I bring upon Pharaoh, and upon Egypt;

afterwards he will let you go hence; when he shall let you go, he shall surely thrust you out hence altogether.

**2.** Speak now in the ears of the people, and let them ask every man of his neighbour, and every woman of her neighbour, jewels of silver, and jewels of gold.

**3.** And the LORD gave the people favour in the sight of the Egyptians. Moreover, the man Moses was very great in the land of Egypt, in the sight of Pharaoh's servants, and in the sight of the people.

**4.** And Moses said: Thus, saith the LORD: About midnight will I go out into the midst of Egypt;

**5.** And all the first-born in the land of Egypt shall die, from the first-born of Pharaoh that sitteth upon his throne, even unto the first-born of the maid-servant that is behind the mill; and all the first-born of cattle.

**6.** And there shall be a great cry throughout all the land of Egypt, such as there hath been none like it, nor shall be like it any more.

**7.** But against any of the children of Israel shall not a dog whet his tongue, against man or beast; that ye may know how that the LORD doth put a difference between the Egyptians and Israel.

**8.** And all these thy servants shall come down unto me, and bow down unto me, saying: Get thee out, and all the people that follow thee; and after that I will go out. And he went out from Pharaoh in hot anger.

**9.** And  the  LORD said unto Moses: Pharaoh will not  hearken  unto  you; that  My  wonders may be multiplied in the land of Egypt.

**10.** And Moses and Aaron did all these wonders before Pharaoh; and the LORD hardened Pharaoh's heart, and he did not let the children of Israel go out of his land.

## Chapter 12

**1.** And the LORD spoke unto Moses and Aaron in the land of Egypt, saying:

**2.** This month shall be unto you the beginning of months; it shall be the first month of the year to you.

**3.** Speak ye unto all the congregation of Israel, saying: In the tenth day of this month they shall take to them every man a lamb, according to their fathers houses, a lamb for a household;

**4.** And if the household be too little for a lamb, then shall he and his neighbour next unto his house take one according to the number of the souls; according to every man's eating ye shall make your count for the lamb.

**5.** Your lamb shall be without blemish, a male of the first year; ye shall take it from the sheep, or from the goats;

**6.** And ye shall keep it unto the fourteenth day of the same month; and the whole assembly of the congregation of Israel shall kill it at dusk.

**7.** And they shall take of the blood, and put it on the two side-posts and on the lintel, upon the houses wherein they shall eat it.

**8.** And they shall eat the flesh in that night, roast with fire, and unleavened bread; with bitter herbs they shall eat it.

**9.** Eat not of it raw, nor sodden at all with water, but roast with fire; its head with its legs and with the inwards thereof.

**10.** And ye shall let nothing of it remain until the morning; but that which remaineth of it until the morning ye shall burn with fire.

**11.** And thus, shall ye eat it: with your loins girded, your shoes on your feet, and your staff in your hand; and ye shall eat it in haste - it is the LORD's Passover.

**12.** For I will go through the land of Egypt in that night, and will smite all the first-born in the land of Egypt, both man and beast; and against all the gods of Egypt I will execute judgments: I am the LORD.

**13.** And the blood shall be to you for a token upon the houses where ye are; and when I see the blood, I will pass over you, and there shall no plague be upon you to destroy you, when I smite the land of Egypt.

**14.** And this day shall be unto you for a memorial, and ye shall keep it a feast to the LORD; throughout your generations ye shall keep it a feast by an ordinance for ever.

**15.** Seven days shall ye eat unleavened bread; howbeit the first day ye shall put away leaven out of your houses; for whosoever eateth leavened bread from the first day until the seventh day, that soul shall be cut off from Israel.

**16.** And in the first day there shall be to you a holy convocation, and in the seventh day a holy convocation; no manner of work shall be done in them, save that which every man must eat, that only may be done by you.

**17.** And ye shall observe the feast of unleavened bread; for in this selfsame day have I brought your hosts out of the land of Egypt; therefore, shall ye observe this day throughout your generations by an ordinance for ever.

**18.** In the first month, on the fourteenth day of the month at even, ye shall eat unleavened bread, until the one and twentieth day of the month at even.

**19.** Seven days shall there be no leaven found in your houses; for whosoever eateth that which is leavened, that soul shall be cut off from the congregation of Israel, whether he be a sojourner, or one that is born in the land.

**20.** Ye shall eat nothing leavened; in all your habitations shall ye eat unleavened bread.

**21.** Then Moses called for all the elders of Israel, and said unto them: Draw out, and take you lambs according to your families, and kill the Passover lamb.

**22.** And ye shall take a bunch of hyssop, and dip it in the blood that is in the basin, and strike the lintel and the two side-posts with the blood that is in the basin; and none of you shall  go out of the door of his house until the morning.

**23.** For the LORD will pass through to smite the Egyptians; and when He seeth the blood upon the lintel, and on the two side-posts, the LORD will pass over the door, and will not suffer the destroyer to come in unto your houses to smite you.

**24.** And ye shall observe this thing for an ordinance to thee and to thy sons for ever.

**25.** And it shall come to pass, when ye be come to the land which the LORD will give you, according as He hath promised, that ye shall keep this service.

**26.** And it shall come to pass, when your children shall say unto you: What mean ye by this service?

**27.** That ye shall say: It is the sacrifice of the LORD's Passover, for that He passed over the houses of the children of Israel in Egypt, when He smote the Egyptians, and delivered our houses. And the people bowed the head and worshipped.

**28.** And the children of Israel went and did so; as the LORD had commanded Moses and Aaron, so did they.

**29.** And it came to pass at midnight, that the LORD smote all the firstborn in the land of Egypt, from the first-born of Pharaoh that sat on his throne unto the first-born of the captive that was in the dungeon; and all the first-born of cattle.

**30.** And Pharaoh rose up in the night, he, and all his servants, and all the Egyptians; and there was a great cry in Egypt; for there was not a house where there was not one dead.

**31.** And he called for Moses and Aaron by night and said: Rise up, get you forth from among my people, both ye and the children of Israel; and go, serve the LORD, as ye have said.

**32.** Take both your flocks and your herds, as ye have said, and be gone; and bless me also.

**33.** And the Egyptians were urgent upon the people, to send them out of the land in haste; for they said: We are all dead men.

**34.** And the people took their dough before it was leavened, their kneading-troughs being bound up in their clothes upon their shoulders.

**35.** And the children of Israel did according to the word of Moses; and they asked of the Egyptians jewels of silver, and jewels of gold, and raiment.

**36.** And the LORD gave the people favour in the sight of the Egyptians, so that they let them have what they asked. And they despoiled the Egyptians.

**37.** And the children of Israel journeyed from Rameses to Succoth, about six hundred thousand men on foot, beside children.

**38.** And a mixed multitude went up also with them; and flocks, and herds, even very much cattle.

**39.** And they baked unleavened cakes of the dough which they brought forth out of Egypt, for it was not leavened; because they were thrust out of Egypt, and could not tarry, neither had they prepared for themselves any victual.

**40.** Now the time that the children of Israel dwelt in Egypt was four hundred and thirty years.

**41.** And it came to pass at the end of four hundred and thirty years, even the selfsame day it came to pass, that all the host of the LORD went out from the land of Egypt.

**42.** It was a night of watching unto the LORD for bringing them out from the land of Egypt; this same night is a night of watching unto the LORD for all the children of Israel throughout their generations.

**43.** And the LORD said unto Moses and Aaron: This is the ordinance of the Passover: there shall no alien eat thereof;

**44.** But every man's servant that is bought for money, when thou hast circumcised him, then shall he eat thereof.

**45.** A sojourner and a hired servant shall not eat thereof.

**46.** In one house shall it be eaten; thou shalt not carry forth aught of the flesh abroad out of the house; neither shall ye break a bone thereof.

**47.** All the congregation of Israel shall keep it.

**48.** And when a stranger shall sojourn with thee, and will keep the Passover to the LORD, let all his males be circumcised, and then let him come near and keep it; and he shall be as one that is born in the land; but no uncircumcised person shall eat thereof.

**49.** One law shall be to him that is homeborn, and unto the stranger that sojourneth among you.

**50.** Thus did all the children of Israel; as the LORD commanded Moses and Aaron, so did they.

**51.** And it came to pass the selfsame day that the LORD did bring the children of Israel out of the land of Egypt by their hosts.

## Chapter 13

**1.** And the LORD spoke unto Moses, saying:

**2.** Sanctify unto Me all the first-born, whatsoever opens the womb among the children of Israel, both of man and of beast, it is Mine.

**3.** And Moses said unto the people: Remember this day, in which ye came out from Egypt, out of the house of bondage; for by strength of hand the LORD brought you out from this place; there shall no leavened bread be eaten.

**4.** This day ye go forth in the month **Abib** [Spring].

**5.** And it shall be when the LORD shall bring thee into the land of the Canaanite, and the Hittite, and the Amorite, and the Hivite, and the Jebusite, which He swore unto thy fathers to give thee, a land flowing with milk and honey, that thou shalt keep this service in this month.

**6.** Seven days thou shalt eat unleavened bread, and in the seventh day shall be a feast to the LORD.

**7.** Unleavened bread shall be eaten throughout the seven days; and there shall no leavened bread be seen with thee, neither shall there be leaven seen with thee, in all thy borders.

**8.** And thou shalt tell thy son in that day, saying: It is because of that which the LORD did for me when I came forth out of Egypt.

**9.** And it shall be for a sign unto thee upon thy hand, and for a memorial between thine eyes, that the law of the LORD may be in thy mouth; for with a strong hand hath the LORD brought thee out of Egypt.

**10.** Thou shalt therefore keep this ordinance in its season from year to year.

**11.** And it shall be when the LORD shall bring thee into the land of the Canaanite, as He swore unto thee and to thy fathers, and shall give it thee,

**12.** That thou shalt set apart unto the LORD all that openeth the womb; every firstling that is a male, which thou hast coming of a beast, shall be the LORD's.

**13.** And every firstling of an ass thou shalt redeem with a lamb; and if thou wilt not redeem it, then thou shalt break its neck; and all the first-born of man among thy sons shalt thou redeem.

**14.** And it shall be when thy son asketh thee in time to come, saying: What is this? that thou shalt say unto him: By strength of hand the LORD brought us out from Egypt, from the house of bondage;

**15.** And it came to pass, when Pharaoh would hardly let us go that the LORD slew all the firstborn in the land of Egypt, both the first-born of man, and the first-born of beast; therefore, I sacrifice to the LORD all that openeth the womb, being males; but all the first-born of my sons I redeem.

**16.** And it shall be for a sign upon thy hand, and for frontlets between your eyes; for by strength of hand the LORD brought us forth out of Egypt.

## Beshalach

**17.** And it came to pass, when Pharaoh had let the people go, that God led them not by the way of the land of the Philistines, although that was near; for God said: 'Lest the people regret when they see war, and they return to Egypt.

**18.** But God led the people about, by the way of the wilderness by the Red Sea; and the children of Israel went up armed out of the land of Egypt.

**19.** And Moses took the bones of Joseph with him; for he had surely sworn the children of Israel, saying: God will surely remember you; and ye shall carry up my bones away hence with you.

**20.** And they took their journey from Succoth, and encamped in Etham, in the edge of the wilderness.

**21.** And the LORD went before them by day in a pillar of cloud, to lead them the way; and by night in a pillar of fire, to give them light; that they might go by day and by night:

**22.** The pillar of cloud by day, and the pillar of fire by night, departed not from before the people.

## Chapter 14

**1.** And the LORD spoke unto Moses, saying:

**2.** Speak unto the children of Israel, that they turn back and encamp before Pi-hahiroth, between Migdol and the sea, before Baal-zephon, over against it shall ye encamp by the sea.

**3.** And Pharaoh will say of the children of Israel: They are entangled in the land, the wilderness hath shut them in.

**4.** And I will harden Pharaoh's heart, and he shall follow after them; and I will get Me honour upon Pharaoh, and upon all his host; and the Egyptians shall know that I am the LORD. And they did so.

**5.** And it was told the king of Egypt that the people were fled; and the heart of Pharaoh and of his servants was turned towards the people, and they said: What is this we have done, that we have let Israel go from serving us?

**6.** And he made ready his chariots, and took his people with him.

**7.** And he took six hundred chosen chariots, and all the chariots of Egypt, and captains over all of them.

**8.** And the LORD hardened the heart of Pharaoh king of Egypt, and he pursued after the children of Israel; for the children of Israel went out with a high hand.

**9.** And the Egyptians pursued after them, all the horses and chariots of Pharaoh, and his horsemen, and his army, and overtook them encamping by the sea, beside Pi-hahiroth, in front of Baal-zephon.

**10.** And when Pharaoh drew nigh, the children of Israel lifted up their eyes, and, behold, the Egyptians were marching after them; and they were sore afraid; and the children of Israel cried out unto the LORD.

**11.** And they said unto Moses: Because there were no graves in Egypt, hast thou taken us away to die in the wilderness? wherefore hast thou dealt thus with us, to bring us forth out of Egypt?

**12.** Is not this the word that we spoke unto thee in Egypt, saying: Let us alone, that we may serve the Egyptians? For it were better for us to serve the Egyptians, than that we should die in the wilderness.

**13.** And Moses said unto the people: Fear ye not, stand still, and see the salvation of the LORD, which He will work for you to-day; for whereas ye have seen the Egyptians to-day, ye shall see them again no more for ever.

**14.** The LORD will fight for you, and ye shall hold your peace.

**15.** And the LORD said unto Moses: Wherefore criest thou unto Me? speak unto the children of Israel, that they go forward.

**16.** And lift thou up thy rod, and stretch out thy hand over the sea, and divide it; and the children of Israel shall go into the midst of the sea on dry ground.

**17.** And I, behold, I will harden the hearts of the Egyptians, and they shall go in after them; and I will get Me honour upon Pharaoh, and upon all his host, upon his chariots, and upon his horsemen.

**18.** And the Egyptians shall know that I am the LORD, when I have gotten Me honour upon Pharaoh, upon his chariots, and upon his horsemen.

**19.** And the angel of God, who went before the camp of Israel, removed and went behind them; and the pillar of cloud removed from before them, and stood behind them;

**20.** And it came between the camp of Egypt and the camp of Israel; and there was the cloud and the darkness here, yet gave it light by night there; and the one came not near the other all the night.

**21.** And Moses stretched out his hand over the sea; and the LORD caused the sea to go back by a strong east wind all the night, and made the sea dry land, and the waters were divided.

**22.** And the children of Israel went into the midst of the sea upon the dry ground; and the waters were a wall unto them on their right hand, and on their left.

**23.** And the Egyptians pursued, and went in after them into the midst of the sea, all Pharaoh's horses, his chariots, and his horsemen.

**24.** And it came to pass in the morning watch, that the LORD looked forth upon the host of the Egyptians through the pillar of fire and of cloud, and discomfited the host of the Egyptians.

**25.** And He took off their chariot wheels, and made them to drive heavily; so that the Egyptians said: Let us flee from the face of Israel; for the LORD fighteth for them against the Egyptians.

**26.** And the LORD said unto Moses: Stretch out thy hand over the sea, that the waters may come back upon the Egyptians, upon their chariots, and upon their horsemen.

**27.** And Moses stretched forth his hand over the sea, and the sea returned to its strength when the morning appeared; and the Egyptians fled against it; and the LORD overthrew the Egyptians in the midst of the sea.

**28.** And the waters returned, and covered the chariots, and the horsemen, even all the host of Pharaoh that went in after them into the sea; there remained not so much as one of them.

**29.** But the children of Israel walked upon dry land in the midst of the sea; and the waters were a wall unto them on their right hand, and on their left.

**30.** Thus, the LORD saved Israel that day out of the hand of the Egyptians; and Israel saw the Egyptians dead upon the sea-shore.

**31.** And Israel saw the great work which the LORD did upon the Egyptians, and the people feared the LORD; and they believed in the LORD, and in His servant Moses.

## Chapter 15

**1.** Then sang Moses and the children of Israel this song unto the LORD, and spoke, saying: I will sing unto the LORD, for He is highly exalted; The horse and his rider hath He thrown into the sea.

**2.** The LORD is my strength and song, And He is become my salvation; This is my God, and I will glorify Him; My father's God, and I will exalt Him.

**3.** The LORD is a man of war, The LORD is His name.

**4.** Pharaoh's chariots and his host hath He cast into the sea, and his chosen captains are sunk in the Red Sea.

**5.** The deeps cover them - They went down into the depths like a stone.

**6.** Thy right hand, O LORD, glorious in power, Thy right hand, O LORD, dasheth in pieces the enemy.

**7.** And in the greatness of Thine excellency Thou overthrowest them that rise up against Thee; Thou sendest forth Thy wrath, it consumeth them as stubble.

**8.** And with the blast of Thy nostrils the waters were piled up - The floods stood upright as a heap; The deeps were congealed in the heart of the sea.

**9.** The enemy said: I will pursue, I will overtake, I will divide the spoil; My lust shall be satisfied upon them; I will draw my sword, my hand shall destroy them.

**10.** Thou didst blow with Thy wind, the sea covered them; They sank as lead in the mighty waters.

**11.** Who is like unto Thee, O LORD, among the mighty? Who is like unto Thee, glorious in holiness, Fearful in praises, doing wonders?

**12.** Thou stretchedst out Thy right hand - The earth

swallowed them.

**13.** Thou in Thy love hast led the people that Thou hast redeemed; Thou hast guided them in Thy strength to Thy holy habitation.

**14.** The peoples have heard, they tremble; Pangs have taken hold on the inhabitants of Philistia.

**15.** Then were the chiefs of Edom affrighted; The mighty men of Moab, trembling taketh hold upon them; All the inhabitants of Canaan are melted away.

**16.** Terror and dread falleth upon them; By the greatness of Thine arm they are as still as a stone; Till Thy people pass over, O LORD, Till the people pass over that Thou hast gotten.

**17.** Thou bringest them in, and plantest them in the mountain of Thine inheritance, the place, O LORD, which Thou hast made for Thee to dwell in, the sanctuary, O Lord, which Thy hands have established.

**18.** The LORD shall reign for ever and ever.

**19.** For the horses of Pharaoh went in with his chariots and with his horsemen into the sea, and the LORD brought back the waters of the sea upon them; but the children of Israel walked on dry land in the midst of the sea.

**20.** And Miriam the prophetess, the sister of Aaron, took a timbrel in her hand; and all the women went out after her with timbrels and with dances.

**21.** And Miriam sang unto them: Sing ye to the LORD, for He  is highly exalted: The horse and his rider hath He thrown into the sea.

**22.** And Moses led Israel onward from the Red Sea, and they went out into the wilderness of Shur; and they went three days in the wilderness, and found no water.

**23.** And when they came to Marah, they could not drink of the waters of Marah, for they were bitter. Therefore, the name of it was called Marah.

**24.** And the people murmured against Moses, saying: What shall we drink?

**25.** And he cried unto the LORD; and the LORD showed him a tree, and he cast it into the waters, and the waters were made sweet. There He made for them a statute and an ordinance, and there He proved them;

**26.** And He said: If thou wilt diligently hearken to the voice of the LORD thy God, and wilt do that which is right in His eyes, and wilt give ear to His commandments, and keep all His statutes, I will put none of the diseases upon thee, which I have put upon the Egyptians; for I am the LORD that healeth thee.

**27.** And they came to Elim, where were twelve springs of water, and three score and ten palm-trees; and they encamped there by the waters.

## Chapter 16

**1.** And they took their journey from Elim, and all the congregation of the children of Israel came unto the wilderness of Sin, which is between Elim and Sinai, on the  fifteenth  day of  the second month after their departing out of the land of Egypt.

**2.** And the whole congregation of the children of Israel murmured against Moses and against Aaron in the wilderness;

**3.** And the children of Israel said unto them: Would that we had died by the hand of the LORD in the land of Egypt, when we sat by the flesh-pots, when we did eat bread to the full; for ye have brought us forth into this wilderness, to kill this whole assembly with hunger.

**4.** Then said the LORD unto Moses: Behold, I will cause to rain bread from heaven for you; and the people shall go out and gather a day's portion every day, that I may prove them, whether they will walk in My law, or not.

**5.** And it shall come to pass on the sixth day that they shall prepare that which they bring in, and it shall be twice as much as they gather daily.

**6.** And Moses and Aaron said unto all the children of Israel: At even, then ye shall know that the LORD hath brought you out from the land of Egypt;

**7.** And in the morning, then ye shall see the glory of the LORD; for that He hath heard your murmurings against the LORD; and what are we, that ye murmur against us?

**8.** And Moses said: This shall be, when the LORD shall give you in the evening flesh to eat, and in the morning bread to the full; for that the LORD heareth your murmurings which ye murmur against Him; and what are we? your murmurings are not against us, but against the LORD.

**9.** And Moses said unto Aaron: Say unto all the congregation of the children of Israel: Come near before the LORD; for He hath heard your murmurings.

**10.** And it came to pass, as Aaron spoke unto the whole congregation of the children of Israel, that they looked toward the wilderness, and, behold, the glory of the LORD appeared in the cloud.

**11.** And the LORD spoke unto Moses, saying:

**12.** I have heard the murmurings of the children of Israel. Speak unto them, saying: At dusk ye shall eat flesh, and in the morning ye shall be filled with bread; and ye shall know that I am the LORD your God.

**13.** And it came to pass at even, that the quails came up, and covered the camp; and in the morning there was a layer of dew round about the camp.

**14.** And when the layer of dew was gone up, behold upon the face of the wilderness a fine, scale-like thing, fine as the hoar-frost on the ground.

**15.** And when the children of Israel saw it, they said one to another: What is it? - for they knew not what it was. And Moses said unto them: It is the bread which the LORD hath given you to eat.

**16.** This is the thing which the LORD hath commanded: Gather ye of it every man according to his eating; an Omer a head, according to the number of your persons, shall ye take it, every man for them that are in his tent.

**17.** And the children of Israel did so, and gathered some more, some less.

**18.** And when they did mete it with an Omer, he that gathered much had nothing over, and he that gathered little had no lack; they gathered every man according to his eating.

**19.** And Moses said unto them: Let no man leave of it till the morning.

**20.** Notwithstanding they hearkened not unto Moses; but some of them left of it until the morning, and it bred worms, and rotted; and Moses was wroth with them.

**21.** And they gathered it morning by morning, every man according to his eating; and as the sun waxed hot, it melted.

**22.** And it came to pass that on the sixth day they gathered twice as much bread, two Omers for each one; and all the rulers of the congregation came and told Moses.

**23.** And he said unto them: This is that which the LORD hath spoken: To-morrow is a solemn rest, a holy sabbath unto the LORD. Bake that which ye will bake, and seethe that which ye will seethe; and all that remaineth over lay up for you to be kept until the morning.

**24.** And they laid it up till the morning, as Moses bade; and it did not rot, neither was there any worm therein.

**25.** And Moses said: Eat that to-day; for to-day is a sabbath unto the LORD; to-day ye shall not find it in the field.

**26.** Six days ye shall gather it; but on the seventh day is the sabbath, in it there shall be none.

**27.** And it came to pass on the seventh day, that there went out some of the people to gather, and they found none.

**28.** And the LORD said unto Moses: How long refuse ye to keep My commandments and My laws?

**29.** See that the LORD hath given you the sabbath; therefore, He giveth you on the sixth day the bread of two days; abide ye every man in his place, let no man go out of his place on the seventh day.

**30.** So, the people rested on the seventh day.

**31.** And the house of Israel called the name thereof Manna; and it was like coriander seed, white; and the taste of it was like wafers made with honey.

**32.** And Moses said: This is the thing which the LORD hath commanded: Let an Omerful of it be kept throughout your generations; that they may see the bread wherewith I fed you in the wilderness, when I brought you forth from the land of Egypt.

**33.** And Moses said unto Aaron: Take a jar, and put an Omerful of manna therein, and lay it up before the LORD, to be kept throughout your generations.

**34.** As the LORD commanded Moses, so Aaron laid it up before the Testimony, to be kept.

**35.** And  the children of Israel did eat the manna forty

years, until they came to a land inhabited; they did eat the manna, until they came unto the borders of the land of Canaan.

**36.** Now an Omer is the tenth part of an ephah.

## Chapter 17

**1.** And all the congregation of the children of Israel journeyed from the wilderness of Sin, by their stages, according to the commandment of the LORD, and encamped in Rephidim; and there was no water for the people to drink.

**2.** Wherefore the people strove with Moses, and said: Give us water that we may drink. And Moses said unto them: Why strive ye with me? wherefore do ye try the LORD?

**3.** And the people thirsted there for water; and the people murmured against Moses, and said: Wherefore hast thou brought us up out of Egypt, to kill us and our children and our cattle with thirst?

**4.** And Moses cried unto the LORD, saying: What shall I do unto this people? they are almost ready to stone me.

**5.** And the LORD said unto Moses: Pass on before the people, and take with thee of the elders of Israel; and thy rod, wherewith thou smotest the river, take in thy hand, and go.

**6.** Behold, I will stand before thee there upon the rock in Horeb; and thou shalt smite the rock, and there shall  come water  out of it, that the people may drink.

And Moses did so in the sight of the elders of Israel.

**7.** And the name of the place was called Massah, and Meribah, because of the striving of the children of Israel, and because they tried the LORD, saying: Is the LORD among us, or not?

**8.** Then came Amalek, and fought with Israel in Rephidim.

**9.** And Moses said unto Joshua: Choose us out men, and go out, fight with Amalek; tomorrow I will stand on the top of the hill with the rod of God in my hand.

**10.** So, Joshua did as Moses had said to him, and fought with Amalek; and Moses, Aaron, and Hur went up to the top of the hill.

**11.** And it came to pass, when Moses held up his hand, that Israel prevailed; and when he let down his hand, Amalek prevailed.

**12.** But Moses - hands were heavy; and they took a stone, and put it under him, and he sat thereon; and Aaron and Hur stayed up his hands, the one on the one side, and the other on the other side; and his hands were steady until the going down of the sun.

**13.** And Joshua discomfited Amalek and his people with the edge of the sword.

**14.** And the LORD said unto Moses: Write this for a memorial in the book, and rehearse it in the ears of Joshua: for I will utterly blot out the remembrance of Amalek from under heaven.

**15.** And Moses built an altar, and called the name of its **Adonai-nissi** [God-miraculous].

**16.** And he said: The hand upon the throne of the LORD: the LORD will have war with Amalek from generation to generation.

## Yitro

## Chapter 18

**1.** Now Jethro, the priest of Midian, Moses' father-in-law, heard of all that God had done for Moses, and for Israel His people, how that the LORD had brought Israel out of Egypt.

**2.** And Jethro Moses father-in-law, took Zipporah, Moses' wife, after he had sent her away,

**3.** And her two sons; of whom the name of the one was Gershom; for he said: I have been a stranger in a strange land;

**4.** And the name of the other was Eliezer: for the God of my father was my help, and delivered me from the sword of Pharaoh.

**5.** And Jethro Moses father-in-law, came with his sons and his wife unto Moses into the wilderness where he was encamped, at the mount of God;

**6.** And he said unto Moses: I thy father-in-law Jethro am coming unto thee, and thy wife, and her two sons with her.

**7.** And Moses went out to meet his father-in-law, and bowed down and kissed him; and they asked each other of their welfare; and they came into the tent.

**8.** And Moses told his father-in-law all that the LORD

had done unto Pharaoh and to the Egyptians for Israel's sake, all the travail that had come upon them by the way, and how the LORD delivered them.

**9.** And Jethro rejoiced for all the goodness which the LORD had done to Israel, in that He had delivered them out of the hand of the Egyptians.

**10.** And Jethro said: Blessed be the LORD, who hath delivered you out of the hand of the Egyptians, and out of the hand of Pharaoh; who hath delivered the people from under the hand of the Egyptians.

**11.** Now I know that the LORD is greater than all gods; yea, for that they dealt proudly against them.

**12.** And Jethro, Moses' father-in-law, took a burnt-offering and sacrifices for God; and Aaron came, and all the elders of Israel, to eat bread with Moses' father-in-law before God.

**13.** And it came to pass on the morrow, that Moses sat to judge the people; and the people stood about Moses from the morning unto the evening.

**14.** And when Moses father-in-law saw all that, he did to the people, he said: What is this thing that thou doest to the people? why sittest thou thyself alone, and all the people stand about thee from morning unto even?

**15.** And Moses said unto his father-in-law: Because the people come unto me to inquire of God;

**16.** When they have a matter, it cometh unto me; and I judge between a man and his neighbour, and I make them know the statutes of God, and His laws.

**17.** And Moses father-in-law said unto him: The thing that thou doest is not good.

**18.** Thou wilt surely wear away, both thou, and this people that is with thee; for the thing is too heavy for thee; thou art not able to perform it thyself alone.

**19.** Hearken now unto my voice, I will give thee counsel, and God be with thee: be thou for the people before God, and bring thou the causes unto God.

**20.** And thou shalt teach them the statutes and the laws, and shalt show them the way wherein they must walk, and the work that they must do.

**21.** Moreover, thou shalt provide out of all the people able men, such as fear God, men of truth, hating unjust gain; and place such over them, to be rulers of thousands, rulers of hundreds, rulers of fifties, and rulers of tens.

**22.** And let them judge the people at all seasons; and it shall be, that every great matter they shall bring unto thee, but every small matter they shall judge themselves; so, shall they make it easier for thee and bear the burden with thee.

**23.** If thou shalt do this thing, and God command thee so, then thou shalt be able to endure, and all this people also shall go to their place in peace.

**24.** So, Moses hearkened to the voice of his father-in-law, and did all that he had said.

**25.** And Moses chose able men out of all Israel, and made them heads over the people, rulers of thousands, rulers of hundreds, rulers of fifties, and rulers of tens.

**26.** And they judged the people at all seasons: the hard causes they brought unto Moses, but every small matter they judged themselves.

**27.** And Moses let his father-in-law depart; and he went his way into his own land.

## Chapter 19

**1.** In the third month after the children of Israel were gone forth out of the land of Egypt, the same day came they into the wilderness of Sinai.

**2.** And when they were departed from Rephidim, and were come to the wilderness of Sinai, they encamped in the wilderness; and there Israel encamped before the mount.

**3.** And Moses went up unto God, and the LORD called unto him out of the mountain, saying: Thus, shalt thou say to the house of Jacob, and tell the children of Israel:

**4.** Ye have seen what I did unto the Egyptians, and how I bore you on eagle's wings, and brought you unto Myself.

**5.** Now therefore, if ye will hearken unto My voice indeed, and keep My covenant, then ye shall be Mine own treasure from among all peoples; for all the earth is Mine;

**6.** And ye shall be unto Me a kingdom of priests, and a holy nation. These are the words which thou shalt speak unto the children of Israel.

**7.** And Moses came and called for the elders of the

people, and set before them all these words which the LORD commanded him.

**8.** And all the people answered together, and said: All that the LORD hath spoken we will do. And Moses reported the words of the people unto the LORD.

**9.** And the LORD said unto Moses: Lo, I come unto thee in a thick cloud, that the people may hear when I speak with thee, and may also believe thee for ever. And Moses told the words of the people unto the LORD.

**10.** And the LORD said unto Moses: Go unto the people, and sanctify them to-day and to-morrow, and let them wash their garments,

**11.** And be ready against the third day; for the third day the LORD will come down in the sight of all the people upon mount Sinai.

**12.** And thou shalt set bounds unto the people round about, saying: Take heed to yourselves, that ye go not up into the mount, or touch the border of it; whosoever toucheth the mount shall be surely put to death;

**13.** No hand shall touch him, but he shall surely be stoned, or shot through; whether it be beast or man, it shall not live; when the ram's horn soundeth long, they shall come up to the mount.

**14.** And Moses went down from the mount unto the people, and sanctified the people; and they washed their garments.

**15.** And he  said unto the people: Be ready against the

third day; come not near a woman.

**16.** And it came to pass on the third day, when it was morning, that there were thunders and lightnings and a thick cloud upon the mount, and the voice of a horn exceeding loud; and all the people that were in the camp trembled.

**17.** And Moses brought forth the people out of the camp to meet God; and they stood at the nether part of the mount.

**18.** Now mount Sinai was altogether on smoke, because the LORD descended upon it in fire; and the smoke thereof ascended as the smoke of a furnace, and the whole mount quaked greatly.

**19.** And when the voice of the horn waxed louder and louder, Moses spoke, and God answered him by a voice.

**20.** And the LORD came down upon mount Sinai, to the top of the mount; and the LORD called Moses to the top of the mount; and Moses went up.

**21.** And the LORD said unto Moses: Go down, charge the people, lest they break through unto the LORD to gaze, and many of them perish.

**22.** And let the priests also, that come near to the LORD, sanctify themselves, lest the LORD break forth upon them.

**23.** And Moses said unto the LORD: The people cannot come up to mount Sinai; for thou didst charge us, saying: Set bounds about the mount, and sanctify it.

**24.** And the LORD said unto him: Go, get thee down, and thou shalt come up, thou, and Aaron with thee; but let not the priests and the people break through to come up unto the LORD, lest He break forth upon them.

**25.** So, Moses went down unto the people, and told them.

## Chapter 20

**1.** And God spoke all these words, saying:

**2.** I am the LORD thy God, who brought thee out of the land of Egypt, out of the house of bondage.

**3.** Thou shalt have no other gods before Me.

**4.** Thou shalt not make unto thee a graven image, nor any manner of likeness, of any thing that is in heaven above, or that is in the earth beneath, or that is in the water under the earth;

**5.** Thou shalt not bow down unto them, nor serve them; for I the LORD thy God am a jealous God, visiting the iniquity of the fathers upon the children unto the third and fourth generation of them that hate Me;

**6.** And showing mercy unto the thousandth generation of them that love Me and keep My commandments.

**7.** Thou shalt not take the name of the LORD thy God in vain; for the LORD will not hold him guiltless that taketh His name in vain.

**8.** Remember the sabbath day, to keep it holy.

**9.** Six days shalt thou labour, and do all thy work;

**10.** But the seventh day is a sabbath unto the LORD thy God, in it thou shalt not do any manner of work, thou, nor thy son, nor thy daughter, nor thy man-servant, nor thy maid-servant, nor thy cattle, nor thy stranger that is within thy gates;

**11.** For in six days the LORD made heaven and earth, the sea, and all that in them is, and rested on the seventh day; wherefore the LORD blessed the sabbath day, and hallowed it.

**12.** Honour thy father and thy mother, that thy days may be long upon the land which the LORD thy God giveth thee.

**13.** Thou shalt not murder. Thou shalt not commit adultery. Thou shalt not steal. Thou shalt not bear false witness against thy neighbour.

**14.** Thou shalt not covet thy neighbour's house; thou shalt not covet thy neighbour's wife, nor his man-servant, nor his maid-servant, nor his ox, nor his ass, nor any thing that is thy neighbour's.

**15.** And all the people perceived the thunderings, and the lightnings, and the voice of the horn, and the mountain smoking; and when the people saw it, they trembled, and stood afar off.

**16.** And they said unto Moses: Speak thou with us, and we will hear; but let not God speak with us, lest we die.

**17.** And Moses said unto the people: Fear not; for God is  come to  prove you, and that His fear may be before you, that ye sin not.

**18.** And the people stood afar off; but Moses drew near unto the thick darkness where God was.

**19.** And the LORD said unto Moses: Thus, thou shalt say unto the children of Israel: Ye yourselves have seen that I have talked with you from heaven.

**20.** Ye shall not make with Me gods of silver, or gods of gold, ye shall not make unto you.

**21.** An altar of earth thou shalt make unto Me, and shalt sacrifice thereon thy burnt-offerings, and thy peace-offerings, thy sheep, and thine oxen; in every place where I cause My name to be mentioned I will come unto thee and bless thee.

**22.** And if thou make Me an altar of stone, thou shalt not build it of hewn stones; for if thou lift up thy tool upon it, thou hast profaned it.

**23.** Neither shalt thou go up by steps unto Mine altar, that thy nakedness be not uncovered thereon.

## Mishpatim

## Chapter 21

**1.** Now these are the ordinances which thou shalt set before them.

**2.** If thou buy a Hebrew servant, six years he shall serve; and in the seventh he shall go out free for nothing.

**3.** If he come in by himself, he shall go out by himself; if he be married, then his wife shall go out with him.

**4.** If his master give him a wife, and she bear him sons or daughters; the wife and her children shall be her master's, and he shall go out by himself.

**5.** But if the servant shall plainly say: I love my master, my wife, and my children; I will not go out free;

**6.** Then his master shall bring him unto God, and shall bring him to the door, or unto the door-post; and his master shall bore his ear through with an awl; and he shall serve him for ever.

**7.** And if a man sell his daughter to be a maid-servant, she shall not go out as the men-servants do.

**8.** If she please not her master, who hath espoused her to himself, then shall he let her be redeemed; to sell her unto a foreign people he shall have no power, seeing he hath dealt deceitfully with her.

**9.** And if he espouse her unto his son, he shall deal with her after the manner of daughters.

**10.** If he take him another wife, her food, her raiment, and her conjugal rights, shall he not diminish.

**11.** And if he do not these three unto her, then shall she go out for nothing, without money.

**12.** He that smiteth a man, so that he dieth, shall surely be put to death.

**13.** And if a man lie not in wait, but God cause it to come to hand; then I will appoint thee a place whither he may flee.

**14.** And if a man come presumptuously upon his neighbour, to slay him with guile; thou shalt take him from Mine altar, that he may die.

**15.** And he that smiteth his father, or his mother, shall be surely put to death.

**16.** And he that stealeth a man, and selleth him, or if he be found in his hand, he shall surely be put to death.

**17.** And he that curseth his father or his mother, shall surely be put to death.

**18.** And if men contend, and one smite the other with a stone, or with his fist, and he die not, but keep his bed;

**19.** If he rise again, and walk abroad upon his staff, then shall he that smote him be quit; only he shall pay for the loss of his time, and shall cause him to be thoroughly healed.

**20.** And if a man smite his bondman, or his bondwoman, with a rod, and he die under his hand, he shall surely be punished.

**21.** Notwithstanding if he continue a day or two, he shall not be punished; for he is his money.

**22.** And if men strive together, and hurt a woman with child, so that her fruit depart, and yet no harm follow, he shall be surely fined, according as the woman's husband shall lay upon him; and he shall pay as the judges determine.

**23.** But if any harm follow, then thou shalt give life for life,

**24.** Eye for eye, tooth for tooth, hand for hand, foot for foot,

**25.** Burning for burning, wound for wound, stripe for stripe.

**26.** And if a man smite the eye of his bondman, or the eye of his bondwoman, and destroy it, he shall let him go free for his eye's sake.

**27.** And if he smite out his bondman's tooth, or his bondwoman's tooth, he shall let him go free for his tooth's sake.

**28.** And if an ox gore a man or a woman, that they die, the ox shall be surely stoned, and its flesh shall not be eaten; but the owner of the ox shall be quit.

**29.** But if the ox was wont to gore in time past, and warning hath been given to its owner, and he hath not kept it in, but it hath killed a man or a woman; the ox shall be stoned, and its owner also shall be put to death.

**30.** If there be laid on him a ransom, then he shall give for the redemption of his life whatsoever is laid upon him.

**31.** Whether it have gored a son, or have gored a daughter, according to this judgment shall it be done unto him.

**32.** If the ox gore a bondman or a bondwoman, he shall give unto their master thirty shekels of silver, and the ox shall be stoned.

**33.** And if a man shall open a pit, or if a man shall dig a pit and not cover it, and an ox or an ass fall therein,

**34.** The owner of the pit shall make it good; he shall give money unto the owner of them, and the dead beast shall be his.

**35.** And if one man's ox hurt another's, so that it dieth; then they shall sell the live ox, and divide the price of it; and the dead also they shall divide.

**36.** Or if it be known that the ox was wont to gore in time past, and its owner hath not kept it in; he shall surely pay ox for ox, and the dead beast shall be his own.

**37.** If a man steal an ox, or a sheep, and kill it, or sell it, he shall pay five oxen for an ox, and four sheep for a sheep.

## Chapter 22

**1.** If a thief be found breaking in, and be smitten so that he dieth, there shall be no bloodguiltiness for him.

**2.** If the sun be risen upon him, there shall be bloodguiltiness for him - he shall make restitution; if he have nothing, then he shall be sold for his theft.

**3.** If the theft be found in his hand alive, whether it be ox, or ass, or sheep, he shall pay double.

**4.** If a man cause a field or vineyard to be eaten, and shall let his beast loose, and it feed in another man's field; of the best of his own field, and of the best of his own vineyard, shall he make restitution.

**5.** If fire break out, and catch in thorns, so that the shocks of corn, or the standing corn, or the field are consumed; he that kindled the fire shall surely make restitution.

**6.** If a man deliver unto his neighbour money or stuff to keep, and it be stolen out of the man's house; if the thief be found, he shall pay double.

**7.** If the thief be not found, then the master of the house shall come near unto God, to see whether he have not put his hand unto his neighbour's goods.

**8.** For every matter of trespass, whether it be for ox, for ass, for sheep, for raiment, or for any manner of lost thing, whereof one saith: **This is it**, the cause of both parties shall come before God; he whom God shall condemn shall pay double unto his neighbour.

**9.** If a man deliver unto his neighbour an ass, or an ox, or a sheep, or any beast, to keep, and it die, or be hurt, or driven away, no man seeing it;

**10.** The oath of the LORD shall be between them both, to see whether he have not put his hand unto his neighbour's goods; and the owner thereof shall accept it, and he shall not make restitution.

**11.** But if it be stolen from him, he shall make restitution unto the owner thereof.

**12.** If it be torn in pieces, let him bring it for witness; he shall not make good that which was torn.

**13.** And if a man borrow aught of his neighbour, and it be hurt, or die, the owner thereof not being with it, he shall surely make restitution.

**14.** If the owner thereof be with it, he shall not make it good; if it be a hireling, he loseth his hire.

**15.** And if a man entice a virgin that is not betrothed, and lie with her, he shall surely pay a dowry for her to be his wife.

**16.** If her father utterly refuse to give her unto him, he shall pay money according to the dowry of virgins.

**17.** Thou shalt not suffer a sorceress to live.

**18.** Whosoever lieth with a beast shall surely be put to death.

**19.** He that sacrificeth unto the gods, save unto the LORD only, shall be utterly destroyed.

**20.** And a stranger shalt thou not wrong, neither shalt thou oppress him; for ye were strangers in the land of Egypt.

**21.** Ye shall not afflict any widow, or fatherless child.

**22.** If thou afflict them in any wise - for if they cry at all unto Me, I will surely hear their cry.

**23.** My wrath shall wax hot, and I will kill you with the sword; and your wives shall be widows, and your children fatherless.

**24.** If thou lend money to any of My people, even to the poor with thee, thou shalt not be to him as a creditor; neither shall ye lay upon him interest.

**25.** If thou at all take thy neighbour's garment to pledge, thou shalt restore it unto him by that the sun goeth down;

**26.** For that is his only covering, it is his garment for his skin; wherein shall he sleep? and it shall come to pass, when he crieth unto Me, that I will hear; for I am gracious.

**27.** Thou shalt not revile God, nor curse a ruler of thy people.

**28.** Thou shalt not delay to offer of the fulness of thy harvest, and of the outflow of thy presses. The first-born of thy sons shalt thou give unto Me.

**29.** Likewise, shalt thou do with thine oxen, and with thy sheep; seven days it shall be with its dam; on the eighth day thou shalt give it Me.

**30.** And ye shall be holy men unto Me; therefore, ye shall not eat any flesh that is torn of beasts in the field; ye shall cast it to the dogs.

## Chapter 23

**1.** Thou shalt not utter a false report; put not thy hand with the wicked to be an unrighteous witness.

**2.** Thou shalt not follow a multitude to do evil; neither shalt thou bear witness in a cause to turn aside after a multitude to pervert justice;

**3.** Neither shalt thou favour a poor man in his cause.

**4.** If thou meet thine enemy's ox or his ass going astray, thou shalt surely bring it back to him again.

**5.** If thou see the ass of him that hateth thee lying under its burden, thou shalt forbear to pass by him; thou shalt surely release it with him.

**6.** Thou shalt not wrest the judgment of thy poor in his cause.

**7.** Keep thee far from a false matter; and the innocent and righteous slay thou not; for I will not justify the wicked.

**8.** And   thou   shalt take no gift; for a gift blindeth them that have sight, and perverteth the  words of the righteous.

**9.** And a stranger shalt thou not oppress; for ye know the heart of a stranger, seeing ye were strangers in the land of Egypt.

**10.** And six years thou shalt sow thy land, and gather in the increase thereof;

**11.** But the seventh year thou shalt let it rest and lie fallow, that the poor of thy people may eat; and what they leave the beast of the field shall eat. In like manner thou shalt deal with thy vineyard, and with thy oliveyard.

**12.** Six days thou shalt do thy work, but on the seventh day thou shalt rest; that thine ox and thine ass may have rest, and the son of thy handmaid, and the stranger, may be refreshed.

**13.** And in all things that I have said unto you take ye heed; and make no mention of the name of other gods, neither let it be heard out of thy mouth.

**14.** Three times thou shalt keep a feast unto Me in the year.

**15.** The feast of unleavened bread shalt thou keep; seven days thou shalt eat unleavened bread, as I commanded thee, at the time appointed in the month Abib - for in it thou camest out from Egypt; and none shall appear before Me empty;

**16.** And the feast of harvest, the first-fruits of thy labours, which thou sowest in the field; and the feast of ingathering, at the end of the year, when thou gatherest in thy labours out of the field.

**17.** Three times in the year all thy males shall appear before the Lord GOD.

**18.** Thou shalt not offer the blood of My sacrifice with leavened bread; neither shall the fat of My feast remain all night until the morning.

**19.** The choicest first-fruits of thy land thou shalt bring into the house of the LORD thy God. Thou shalt not seethe a kid in its mother's milk.

**20.** Behold, I send an angel before thee, to keep thee by the way, and to bring thee into the place which I have prepared.

**21.** Take heed of him, and hearken unto his voice; be not rebellious against him; for he will not pardon your transgression; for My name is in him.

**22.** But if thou shalt indeed hearken unto his voice, and do all that I speak; then I will be an enemy unto thine enemies, and an adversary unto thine adversaries.

**23.** For Mine angel shall go before thee, and bring thee in unto the Amorite, and the Hittite, and the Perizzite, and the Canaanite, the Hivite, and the Jebusite; and I will cut them off.

**24.** Thou shalt not bow down to their gods, nor serve them, nor do after their doings; but thou shalt utterly overthrow them, and break in pieces their pillars.

**25.** And ye shall serve the LORD your God, and He will bless thy bread, and thy water; and I will take sickness away from the midst of thee.

**26.** None  shall miscarry, nor  be barren, in thy land;

the number of thy days I will fulfil.

**27.** I will send My terror before thee, and will discomfit all the people to whom thou shalt come, and I will make all thine enemies turn their backs unto thee.

**28.** And I will send the hornet before thee, which shall drive out the Hivite, the Canaanite, and the Hittite, from before thee.

**29.** I will not drive them out from before thee in one year, lest the land become desolate, and the beasts of the field multiply against thee.

**30.** By little and little I will drive them out from before thee, until thou be increased, and inherit the land.

**31.** And I will set thy border from the Red Sea even unto the sea of the Philistines, and from the wilderness unto athe River; for I will deliver the inhabitants of the land into your hand; and thou shalt drive them out before thee.

**32.** Thou shalt make no covenant with them, nor with their gods.

**33.** They shall not dwell in thy land - lest they make thee sin against Me, for thou wilt serve their gods - for they will be a snare unto thee.


## Chapter 24

**1.** And unto Moses He said: Come up unto the LORD, thou, and Aaron, Nadab, and Abihu, and seventy of the elders of Israel; and worship ye afar off;

**2.** And Moses alone shall come near unto the LORD; but they shall not come near; neither shall the people go up with him.

**3.** And Moses came and told the people all the words of the LORD, and all the ordinances; and all the people answered with one voice, and said: All the words which the Lord hath spoken will we do.

**4.** And Moses wrote all the words of the LORD, and rose up early in the morning, and builded an altar under the mount, and twelve pillars, according to the twelve tribes of Israel.

**5.** And he sent the young men of the children of Israel, who offered burnt-offerings, and sacrificed peace-offerings of oxen unto the LORD.

**6.** And Moses took half of the blood, and put it in basins; and half of the blood he dashed against the altar.

**7.** And he took the book of the covenant, and read in the hearing of the people; and they said: All that the LORD hath spoken will we do, and obey.

**8.** And Moses took the blood, and sprinkled it on the people, and said: Behold the blood of the covenant, which the LORD hath made with you in agreement with all these words.

**9.** Then went up Moses, and Aaron, Nadab, and Abihu, and seventy of the elders of Israel;

**10.** And they saw the God of Israel; and there was under His feet the like of a paved work of sapphire stone, and the like of the very heaven for clearness.

**11.** And upon the nobles of the children of Israel He laid not His hand; and they beheld God, and did eat and drink.

**12.** And the LORD said unto Moses: Come up to Me into the mount and be there; and I will give thee the tables of stone, and the law and the commandment, which I have written, that thou mayest teach them.

**13.** And Moses rose up, and Joshua his minister; and Moses went up into the mount of God.

**14.** And unto the elders he said: Tarry ye here for us, until we come back unto you; and, behold, Aaron and Hur are with you; whosoever hath a cause, let him come near unto them.

**15.** And Moses went up into the mount, and the cloud covered the mount.

**16.** And the glory of the LORD abode upon mount Sinai, and the cloud covered it six days; and the seventh day He called unto Moses out of the midst of the cloud.

**17.** And the appearance of the glory of the LORD was like devouring fire on the top of the mount in the eyes of the children of Israel.

**18.** And Moses entered into the midst of the cloud, and went up into the mount; and Moses was in the mount forty days and forty nights.

## Terumah

## Chapter 25

**1.** And the LORD spoke unto Moses, saying:

**2.** Speak unto the children of Israel, that they take for Me an offering; of every man whose heart maketh him willing ye shall take My offering.

**3.** And this is the offering which ye shall take of them: gold, and silver, and brass;

**4.** And blue, and purple, and scarlet, and fine linen, and goats hair;

**5.** And rams skins dyed red, and sealskins, and acacia-wood;

**6.** Oil for the light, spices for the anointing oil, and for the sweet incense;

**7.** Onyx stones, and stones to be set, for the ephod, and for the breastplate.

**8.** And let them make Me a sanctuary, that I may dwell among them.

**9.** According to all that I show thee, the pattern of the tabernacle, and the pattern of all the furniture thereof, even so shall ye make it.

**10.** And they shall make an ark of acacia-wood: two cubits and a half shall be the length thereof, and a cubit and a half the breadth thereof, and a cubit and a half the height thereof.

**11.** And thou shalt overlay it with pure gold, within and without shalt thou overlay it, and shalt make upon it a crown of gold round about.

**12.** And thou shalt cast four rings of gold for it, and put them in the four feet thereof; and two rings shall be on the one side of it, and two rings on the other side of it.

**13.** And thou shalt make staves of acacia-wood, and overlay them with gold.

**14.** And thou shalt put the staves into the rings on the sides of the ark, wherewith to bear the ark.

**15.** The staves shall be in the rings of the ark; they shall not be taken from it.

**16.** And thou shalt put into the ark the testimony which I shall give thee.

**17.** And thou shalt make an ark-cover of pure gold: two cubits and a half shall be the length thereof, and a cubit and a half the breadth thereof.

**18.** And thou shalt make two cherubim of gold; of beaten work shalt thou make them, at the two ends of the ark-cover.

**19.** And make one cherub at the one end, and one cherub at the other end; of one piece with the ark-cover shall ye make the cherubim of the two ends thereof.

**20.** And the cherubim shall spread out their wings on high, screening the ark-cover with their wings, with their faces one to another; toward the ark-cover shall the faces of the cherubim be.

**21.** And thou shalt put the ark-cover above upon the ark; and in the ark thou shalt put the testimony that I shall give thee.

**22.** And there I will meet with thee, and I will speak with thee from above the ark-cover, from between the two cherubim which are upon the ark of the testimony, of all things which I will give thee in commandment unto the children of Israel.

**23.** And thou shalt make a table of acacia-wood: two cubits shall be the length thereof, and a cubit the breadth thereof, and a cubit and a half the height thereof.

**24.** And thou shalt overlay it with pure gold, and make thereto a crown of gold round about.

**25.** And thou shalt make unto it a border of a handbreadth round about, and thou shalt make a golden crown to the border thereof round about.

**26.** And thou shalt make for it four rings of gold, and put the rings in the four corners that are on the four feet thereof.

**27.** Close by the border shall the rings be, for places for the staves to bear the table.

**28.** And thou shalt make the staves of acacia-wood, and overlay them with gold, that the table may be borne with them.

**29.** And thou shalt make the dishes thereof, and the pans thereof, and the jars thereof, and the bowls thereof, wherewith to pour out; of pure gold shalt thou make them.

**30.** And thou shalt set upon the table showbread before Me always.

**31.** And thou shalt make a candlestick of pure gold: of beaten work shall the candlestick be made, even its base, and its shaft; its cups, its knops, and its flowers, shall be of one piece with it.

**32.** And  there shall  be six branches going out of the

sides thereof: three branches of the candlestick out of the one side thereof, and three branches of the candlestick out of the other side thereof;

**33.** Three cups made like almond-blossoms in one branch, a knop and a flower; and three cups made like almond-blossoms in the other branch, a knop and a flower; so, for the six branches going out of the candlestick.

**34.** And in the candlestick four cups made like almond-blossoms, the knops thereof, and the flowers thereof.

**35.** And  a knop  under two branches of one piece with it, and a knop under two branches of one piece with it, and a knop under two branches of one piece with it, for the six branches going out of the candlestick.

**36.** Their knops and their branches shall be of one piece with it; the whole of it one beaten work of pure gold.

**37.** And thou shalt make the lamps thereof, seven; and they shall light the lamps thereof, to give light over against it.

**38.** And the tongs thereof, and the snuffdishes thereof, shall be of pure gold.

**39.** Of a talent of pure gold shall it be made, with all these vessels.

**40.** And see that thou make them after their pattern, which is being shown thee in the mount.

## Chapter 26

**1.** Moreover, thou shalt make the tabernacle with ten curtains: of fine twined linen, and blue, and purple, and scarlet, with cherubim the work of the skilful workman shalt thou make them.

**2.** The length of each curtain shall be eight and twenty cubits, and the breadth of each curtain four cubits; all the curtains shall have one measure.

**3.** Five curtains shall be coupled together one to another; and the other five curtains shall be coupled one to another.

**4.** And thou shalt make loops of blue upon the edge of the one curtain that is outmost in the first set; and likewise, shalt thou make in the edge of the curtain that is outmost in the second set.

**5.** Fifty loops shalt thou make in the one curtain, and fifty loops shalt thou make in the edge of the curtain that is in the second set; the loops shall be opposite one to another.

**6.** And thou shalt make fifty clasps of gold, and couple the curtains one to another with the clasps, that the tabernacle may be one whole.

**7.** And thou shalt make curtains of goats' hair for a tent over the tabernacle; eleven curtains shalt thou make them.

**8.** The length of each curtain shall be thirty cubits, and the breadth of each curtain four cubits; the eleven curtains shall have one measure.

**9.** And thou  shalt couple five curtains by themselves,

and six curtains by themselves, and shalt double over the sixth curtain in the forefront of the tent.

**10.** And thou shalt make fifty loops on the edge of the one curtain that is outmost in the first set, and fifty loops upon the edge of the curtain which is outmost in the second set.

**11.** And thou shalt make fifty clasps of brass, and put the clasps into the loops, and couple the tent together, that it may be one.

**12.** And as for the overhanging part that remaineth of the curtains of the tent, the half curtain that remaineth over shall hang over the back of the tabernacle.

**13.** And the cubit on the one side, and the cubit on the other side, of that which remaineth over in the length of the curtains of the tent, shall hang over the sides of the tabernacle on this side and on that side, to cover it.

**14.** And thou shalt make a covering for the tent of rams' skins dyed red and a covering of sealskins above.

**15.** And thou shalt make the boards for the tabernacle of acacia-wood, standing up.

**16.** Ten cubits shall be the length of a board, and a cubit and a half the breadth of each board.

**17.** Two tenons shall there be in each board, joined one to another; thus, shalt thou make for all the boards of the tabernacle.

**18.** And thou shalt make the boards for the tabernacle, twenty boards for the south side southward:

**19.** And thou shalt make forty sockets of silver under the twenty boards: two sockets under one board for its two tenons, and two sockets under another board for its two tenons;

**20.** And for the second side of the tabernacle, on the north side, twenty boards.

**21.** And their forty sockets of silver: two sockets under one board, and two sockets under another board.

**22.** And for the hinder part of the tabernacle westward thou shalt make six boards.

**23.** And two boards shalt thou make for the corners of the tabernacle in the hinder part.

**24.** And they shall be double beneath, and in like manner they shall be complete unto the top thereof unto the first ring; thus, shall it be for them both; they shall be for the two corners.

**25.** Thus, there shall be eight boards, and their sockets of silver, sixteen sockets: two sockets under one board, and two sockets under another board.

**26.** And thou shalt make bars of acacia-wood: five for the boards of the one side of the tabernacle,

**27.** And five bars for the boards of the other side of the tabernacle, and five bars for the boards of the side of the tabernacle, for the hinder part westward;

**28.** And the middle bar in the midst of the boards, which shall pass through from end to end.

**29.** And thou shalt overlay the boards with gold, and make their rings of gold for holders for the bars; and thou shalt overlay the bars with gold.

**30.** And thou shalt rear up the tabernacle according to the fashion thereof which hath been shown thee in the mount.

**31.** And thou shalt make a veil of blue, and purple, and scarlet, and fine twined linen; with cherubim the work of the skilful workman shall it be made.

**32.** And thou shalt hang it upon four pillars of acacia overlaid with gold, their hooks being of gold, upon four sockets of silver.

**33.** And thou shalt hang up the veil under the clasps, and shalt bring in thither within the veil the ark of the testimony; and the veil shall divide unto you between the holy place and the most holy.

**34.** And thou shalt put the ark-cover upon the ark of the testimony in the most holy place.

**35.** And thou shalt set the table without the veil, and the candlestick over against the table on the side of the tabernacle toward the south; and thou shalt put the table on the north side.

**36.** And thou shalt make a screen for the door of the Tent, of blue, and purple, and scarlet, and fine twined linen, the work of the weaver in colours.

**37.** And thou shalt make for the screen five pillars of acacia, and overlay them with gold; their hooks shall be of gold; and thou shalt cast five sockets of brass for them.

## Chapter 27

**1.** And thou shalt make the altar of acacia-wood, five cubits long, and five cubits broad; the altar shall be four-square; and the height thereof shall be three cubits.

**2.** And thou shalt make the horns of it upon the four corners thereof; the horns thereof shall be of one piece with it; and thou shalt overlay it with brass.

**3.** And thou shalt make its pots to take away its ashes, and its shovels, and its basins, and its flesh-hooks, and its fire-pans; all the vessels thereof thou shalt make of brass.

**4.** And thou shalt make for it a grating of network of brass; and upon the net shalt thou make four brazen rings in the four corners thereof.

**5.** And thou shalt put it under the ledge round the altar beneath, that the net may reach halfway up the altar.

**6.** And thou shalt make staves for the altar, staves of acacia-wood, and overlay them with brass.

**7.** And the staves thereof shall be put into the rings, and the staves shall be upon the two sides of the altar, in bearing it.

**8.** Hollow with planks shalt thou make it; as it hath been shown thee in the mount, so shall they make it.

**9.** And thou shalt make the court of the tabernacle: for the south side southward, there shall be hangings for the court of fine twined linen a hundred cubits long for one side.

**10.** And  the pillars thereof shall be twenty, and their

sockets twenty, of brass; the hooks of the pillars and their fillets shall be of silver.

**11.** And likewise for the north side in length there shall be hangings a hundred cubits long, and the pillars thereof twenty, and their sockets twenty, of brass; the hooks of the pillars and their fillets of silver.

**12.** And for the breadth of the court on the west side shall be hangings of fifty cubits: their pillars ten, and their sockets ten.

**13.** And the breadth of the court on the east side eastward shall be fifty cubits.

**14.** The hangings for the one side [of the gate] shall be fifteen cubits: their pillars three, and their sockets three.

**15.** And for the other side shall be hangings of fifteen cubits: their pillars three, and their sockets three.

**16.** And for the gate of the court shall be a screen of twenty cubits, of blue, and purple, and scarlet, and fine twined linen, the work of the weaver in colours: their pillars four, and their sockets four.

**17.** All the pillars of the court round about shall be filleted with silver; their hooks of silver, and their sockets of brass.

**18.** The length of the court shall be a hundred cubits, and the breadth fifty every where, and the height five cubits, of fine twined linen, and their sockets of brass.

**19.** All the instruments of the tabernacle in all the service thereof, and all the pins thereof, and all the pins of the court, shall be of brass.

## Tetzaveh

**20.** And thou shalt command the children of Israel, that they bring unto thee pure olive oil beaten for the light, to cause a lamp to burn continually.

**21.** In the tent of meeting, without the veil which is before the testimony, Aaron and his sons shall set it in order, to burn from evening to morning before the LORD; it shall be a statute for ever throughout their generations on the behalf of the children of Israel.

## Chapter 28

**1.** And bring thou near unto the Aaron thy brother, and his sons with him, from among the children of Israel, that they may minister unto Me in the priest's office, even Aaron, Nadab and Abihu, Eleazar and Ithamar, Aaron's sons.

**2.** And thou shalt make holy garments for Aaron thy brother, for splendour and for beauty.

**3.** And thou shalt speak unto all that are wise-hearted, whom I have filled with the spirit of wisdom, that they make Aaron's garments to sanctify him, that he may minister unto Me in the priest's office.

**4.** And these are the garments which they shall make: a breastplate, and an ephod, and a robe, and a tunic of chequer work, a mitre, and a girdle; and they shall make holy garments for Aaron thy brother, and his sons, that he may minister unto Me in the priest's office.

**5.** And they shall take the gold, and the blue, and the purple, and the scarlet, and the fine linen.

**6.** And they shall make the ephod of gold, of blue, and purple, scarlet, and fine twined linen, the work of the skilful workman.

**7.** It shall have two shoulder-pieces joined to the two ends thereof, that it may be joined together.

**8.** And the skilfully woven band, which is upon it, wherewith to gird it on, shall be like the work thereof and of the same piece: of gold, of blue, and purple, and scarlet, and fine twined linen.

**9.** And thou shalt take two onyx stones, and grave on them the names of the children of Israel:

**10.** Six of their names on the one stone, and the names of the six that remain on the other stone, according to their birth.

**11.** With the work of an engraver in stone, like the engravings of a signet, shalt thou engrave the two stones, according to the names of the children of Israel; thou shalt make them to be inclosed in settings of gold.

**12.** And thou shalt put the two stones upon the shoulder-pieces of the ephod, to be stones of memorial for the children of Israel; and Aaron shall bear their names before the LORD upon his two shoulders for a memorial.

**13.** And thou shalt make settings of gold;

**14.** And two chains of pure gold; of plaited thread shalt thou make them, of wreathen work; and thou shalt put the wreathen chains on the settings.

**15.** And thou shalt make a breastplate of judgment, the work of the skilful workman; like the work of the ephod, thou shalt make it: of gold, of blue, and purple, and scarlet, and fine twined linen, shalt thou make it.

**16.** Four-square it shall be and double: a span shall be the length thereof, and a span the breadth thereof.

**17.** And thou shalt set in it settings of stones, four rows of stones: a row of carnelian, topaz, and smaragd shall be the first row;

**18.** And the second row a carbuncle, a sapphire, and an emerald;

**19.** And the third row a jacinth, an agate, and an amethyst;

**20.** And the fourth row a beryl, and an onyx, and a jasper; they shall be inclosed in gold in their settings.

**21.** And the stones shall be according to the names of the children of Israel, twelve, according to their names; like the engravings of a signet, every one according to his name, they shall be for the twelve tribes.

**22.** And thou shalt make upon the breastplate plaited chains of wreathen work of pure gold.

**23.** And thou shalt make upon the breastplate two rings of gold, and shalt put the two rings on the two ends of the breastplate.

**24.** And thou shalt put the two wreathen chains of

gold on the two rings at the ends of the breastplate.

**25.** And the other two ends of the two wreathen chains thou shalt put on the two settings, and put them on the shoulder-pieces of the ephod, in the forepart thereof.

**26.** And thou shalt make two rings of gold, and thou shalt put them upon the two ends of the breastplate, upon the edge thereof, which is toward the side of the ephod inward.

**27.** And thou shalt make two rings of gold, and shalt put them on the two shoulder-pieces of the ephod underneath, in the forepart thereof, close by the coupling thereof, above the skilfully woven band of the ephod.

**28.** And they shall bind the breastplate by the rings thereof unto the rings of the ephod with a thread of blue, that it may be upon the skilfully woven band of the ephod, and that the breastplate be not loosed from the ephod.

**29.** And Aaron shall bear the names of the children of Israel in the breastplate of judgment upon his heart, when he goeth in unto the holy place, for a memorial before the LORD continually.

**30.** And thou shalt put in the breastplate of judgment the Urim and the Thummim; and they shall be upon Aaron's heart, when he goeth in before the LORD; and Aaron shall bear the judgment of the children of Israel upon his heart before the LORD continually.

**31.** And thou shalt make the robe of the ephod all of blue.

**32.** And it shall have a hole for the head in the midst thereof; it shall have a binding of woven work round about the hole of it, as it were the hole of a coat of mail that it be not rent.

**33.** And upon the skirts of it thou shalt make pomegranates of blue, and of purple, and of scarlet, round about the skirts thereof; and bells of gold between them round about:

**34.** A golden bell and a pomegranate, a golden bell and a pomegranate, upon the skirts of the robe round about.

**35.** And it shall be upon Aaron to minister; and the sound thereof shall be heard when he goeth in unto the holy place before the LORD, and when he cometh out, that he die not.

**36.** And thou shalt make a plate of pure gold, and engrave upon it, like the engravings of a signet: HOLY TO THE LORD.

**37.** And thou shalt put it on a thread of blue, and it shall be upon the mitre; upon the forefront of the mitre it shall be.

**38.** And it shall be upon Aaron's forehead, and Aaron shall bear the iniquity committed in the holy things, which the children of Israel shall hallow, even in all their holy gifts; and it shall be always upon his forehead, that they may be accepted before the LORD.

**39.** And thou shalt weave the tunic in chequer work of fine linen, and thou shalt make a mitre of fine linen, and thou shalt make a girdle, the work of the weaver in colours.

**40.** And for Aaron's sons thou shalt make tunics, and thou shalt make for them girdles, and head-tires shalt thou make for them, for splendour and for beauty.

**41.** And thou shalt put them upon Aaron thy brother, and upon his sons with him; and shalt anoint them, and consecrate them, and sanctify them, that they may minister unto Me in the priest's office.

**42.** And thou shalt make them linen breeches to cover the flesh of their nakedness; from the loins even unto the thighs they shall reach.

**43.** And they shall be upon Aaron, and upon his sons, when they go in unto the tent of meeting, or when they come near unto the altar to minister in the holy place; that they bear not iniquity, and die; it shall be a statute for ever unto him and unto his seed after him.

## Chapter 29

**1.** And this is the thing that thou shalt do unto them to hallow them, to minister unto Me in the priest's office: take one young bullock and two rams without blemish,

**2.** And unleavened bread, and cakes unleavened mingled with oil, and wafers unleavened spread with oil; of fine wheaten flour shalt thou make them.

**3.** And  thou  shalt put them into one basket, and bring

them in the basket, with the bullock and the two rams.

**4.** And Aaron and his sons thou shalt bring unto the door of the tent of meeting, and shalt wash them with water.

**5.** And thou shalt take the garments, and put upon Aaron the tunic, and the robe of the ephod, and the ephod, and the breastplate, and gird him with the skilfully woven band of the ephod.

**6.** And thou shalt set the mitre upon his head, and put the holy crown upon the mitre.

**7.** Then shalt thou take the anointing oil, and pour it upon his head, and anoint him.

**8.** And thou shalt bring his sons, and put tunics upon them.

**9.** And thou shalt gird them with girdles, Aaron and his sons, and bind head-tires on them; and they shall have the priesthood by a perpetual statute; and thou shalt consecrate Aaron and his sons.

**10.** And thou shalt bring the bullock before the tent of meeting; and Aaron and his sons shall lay their hands upon the head of the bullock.

**11.** And thou shalt kill the bullock before the LORD, at the door of the tent of meeting.

**12.** And thou shalt take of the blood of the bullock, and put it upon the horns of the altar with thy finger; and thou shalt pour out all the remaining blood at the base of the altar.

**13.** And thou shalt take all the fat that covereth the inwards, and the lobe above the liver, and the two kidneys, and the fat that is upon them, and make them smoke upon the altar.

**14.** But the flesh of the bullock, and its skin, and its dung, shalt thou burn with fire without the camp; it is a sin-offering.

**15.** Thou shalt also take the one ram; and Aaron and his sons shall lay their hands upon the head of the ram.

**16.** And thou shalt slay the ram, and thou shalt take its blood, and dash it round about against the altar.

**17.** And thou shalt cut the ram into its pieces, and wash its inwards, and its legs, and put them with its pieces, and with its head.

**18.** And thou shalt make the whole ram smoke upon the altar; it is a burnt-offering unto the LORD; it is a sweet savour, an offering made by fire unto the LORD.

**19.** And thou shalt take the other ram; and Aaron and his sons shall lay their hands upon the head of the ram.

**20.** Then shalt thou kill the ram, and take of its blood, and put it upon the tip of the right ear of Aaron, and upon the tip of the right ear of his sons, and upon the thumb of their right hand, and upon the great toe of their right foot, and dash the blood against the altar round about.

**21.** And thou shalt take of the blood that is upon the altar, and of the anointing oil, and sprinkle it upon Aaron, and upon his garments, and upon his sons, and upon the garments of his sons with him; and he and his garments shall be hallowed, and his sons and his sons' garments with him.

**22.** Also, thou shalt take of the ram the fat, and the fat tail, and the fat that covereth the inwards, and the lobe of the liver, and the two kidneys, and the fat that is upon them, and the right thigh; for it is a ram of consecration;

**23.** And one loaf of bread, and one cake of oiled bread, and one wafer, out of the basket of unleavened bread that is before the LORD.

**24.** And thou shalt put the whole upon the hands of Aaron, and upon the hands of his sons; and shalt wave them for a wave-offering before the LORD.

**25.** And thou shalt take them from their hands, and make them smoke on the altar upon the burnt-offering, for a sweet savour before the LORD; it is an offering made by fire unto the LORD.

**26.** And thou shalt take the breast of Aaron's ram of consecration, and wave it for a wave-offering before the LORD; and it shall be thy portion.

**27.** And thou shalt sanctify the breast of the wave-offering, and the thigh of the heave-offering, which is waved, and which is heaved up, of the ram of consecration, even of that which is Aaron's, and of that which is his sons'.

**28.** And it shall be for Aaron and his sons as a due for ever from the children of Israel; for it is a heave-offering; and it shall be a heave-offering from the children of Israel of their sacrifices of peace-offerings, even their heave-offering unto the LORD.

**29.** And the holy garments of Aaron shall be for his sons after him, to be anointed in them, and to be consecrated in them.

**30.** Seven days shall the son that is priest in his stead put them on, even he who cometh into the tent of meeting to minister in the holy place.

**31.** And thou shalt take the ram of consecration, and seethe its flesh in a holy place.

**32.** And Aaron and his sons shall eat the flesh of the ram, and the bread that is in the basket, at the door of the tent of meeting.

**33.** And they shall eat those things wherewith atonement was made, to consecrate and to sanctify them; but a stranger shall not eat thereof, because they are holy.

**34.** And if aught of the flesh of the consecration, or of the bread, remain unto the morning, then thou shalt burn the remainder with fire; it shall not be eaten, because it is holy.

**35.** And thus, shalt thou do unto Aaron, and to his sons, according to all that I have commanded thee; seven days shalt thou consecrate them.

**36.** And every day shalt thou offer the bullock of sin-offering, beside the other offerings of atonement; and thou shalt do the purification upon the altar when thou makest atonement for it; and thou shalt anoint it, to sanctify it.

**37.** Seven days thou shalt make atonement for the altar, and sanctify it; thus, shall the altar be most holy; whatsoever toucheth the altar shall be holy.

**38.** Now this is that which thou shalt offer upon the altar: two lambs of the first-year day by day continually.

**39.** The one lamb thou shalt offer in the morning; and the other lamb thou shalt offer at dusk.

**40.** And with the one lamb a tenth part of an ephah of fine flour mingled with the fourth part of a hin of beaten oil; and the fourth part of a hin of wine for a drink-offering.

**41.** And the other lamb thou shalt offer at dusk, and shalt do thereto according to the meal-offering of the morning, and according to the drink-offering thereof, for a sweet savour, an offering made by fire unto the LORD.

**42.** It shall be a continual burnt-offering throughout your generations at the door of the tent of meeting before the LORD, where I will meet with you, to speak there unto thee.

**43.** And there I will meet with the children of Israel; and the Tent shall be sanctified by My glory.

**44.** And I will sanctify the tent of meeting, and the altar; Aaron also and his sons will I sanctify, to minister to Me in the priest's office.

**45.** And I will dwell among the children of Israel, and will be their God.

**46.** And they shall know that I am the LORD their

God, that brought them forth out of the land of Egypt, that I may dwell among them. I am the LORD their God.

## Chapter 30

**1.** And thou shalt make an altar to burn incense upon; of acacia-wood shalt thou make it.

**2.** A cubit shall be the length thereof, and a cubit the breadth thereof; foursquare shall it be; and two cubits shall be the height thereof; the horns thereof shall be of one piece with it.

**3.** And thou shalt overlay it with pure gold, the top thereof, and the sides thereof round about, and the horns thereof; and thou shalt make unto it a crown of gold round about.

**4.** And two golden rings shalt thou make for it under the crown thereof, upon the two ribs thereof, upon the two sides of it shalt thou make them; and they shall be for places for staves wherewith to bear it.

**5.** And thou shalt make the staves of acacia-wood, and overlay them with gold.

**6.** And thou shalt put it before the veil that is by the ark of the testimony, before the ark-cover that is over the testimony, where I will meet with thee.

**7.** And Aaron shall burn thereon incense of sweet spices; every morning, when he dresseth the lamps, he shall burn it.

**8.** And when Aaron lighteth the lamps at dusk, he shall  burn it, a perpetual  incense  before the LORD throughout your generations.

**9.** Ye shall offer no strange incense thereon, nor burnt-offering, nor meal-offering; and ye shall pour no drink-offering thereon.

**10.** And Aaron shall make atonement upon the horns of it once in the year; with the blood of the sin-offering of atonement once in the year shall he make atonement for it throughout your generations; it is most holy unto the LORD.

## Ki Tisa

**11.** And the LORD spoke unto Moses, saying:

**12.** When thou takest the sum of the children of Israel, according to their number, then shall they give every man a ransom for his soul unto the LORD, when thou numberest them; that there be no plague among them, when thou numberest them.

**13.** This they shall give, every one that passeth among them that are numbered, half a shekel after the shekel of the sanctuary - the shekel is twenty gerahs - half a shekel for an offering to the LORD.

**14.** Every one that passeth among them that are numbered, from twenty years old and upward, shall give the offering of the LORD.

**15.** The rich shall not give more, and the poor shall not give less, than the half shekel, when they give the offering of the LORD, to make atonement for your souls.

**16.** And thou shalt take the atonement money from the children of Israel, and shalt appoint it for the service of the tent of meeting, that it may be a memorial for the children of Israel before the LORD, to make atonement for your souls.

**17.** And the LORD spoke unto Moses, saying:

**18.** Thou shalt also make a laver of brass, and the base thereof of brass, whereat to wash; and thou shalt put it between the tent of meeting and the altar, and thou shalt put water therein.

**19.** And Aaron and his sons shall wash their hands and their feet thereat;

**20.** When they go into the tent of meeting, they shall wash with water, that they die not; or when they come near to the altar to minister, to cause an offering made by fire to smoke unto the LORD;

**21.** So, they shall wash their hands and their feet, that they die not; and it shall be a statute for ever to them, even to him and to his seed throughout their generations.

**22.** Moreover, the LORD spoke unto Moses, saying:

**23.** Take thou also unto thee the chief spices, of flowing myrrh five hundred shekels, and of sweet cinnamon half so much, even two hundred and fifty, and of sweet calamus two hundred and fifty,

**24.** And of cassia five hundred, after the shekel of the sanctuary, and of olive oil a hin.

**25.** And thou shalt make it a holy anointing oil, a perfume compounded after the art of the perfumer; it shall be a holy anointing oil.

**26.** And thou shalt anoint therewith the tent of meeting, and the ark of the testimony,

**27.** And the table and all the vessels thereof, and the candlestick and the vessels thereof, and the altar of incense,

**28.** And the altar of burnt-offering with all the vessels thereof, and the laver and the base thereof.

**29.** And thou shalt sanctify them, that they may be most holy; whatsoever toucheth them shall be holy.

**30.** And thou shalt anoint Aaron and his sons, and sanctify them, that they may minister unto Me in the priest's office.

**31.** And thou shalt speak unto the children of Israel, saying: This shall be a holy anointing oil unto Me throughout your generations.

**32.** Upon the flesh of man shall it not be poured, neither shall ye make any like it, according to the composition thereof; it is holy, and it shall be holy unto you.

**33.** Whosoever compoundeth any like it, or whosoever putteth any of it upon a stranger, he shall be cut off from his people.

**34.** And the LORD said unto Moses: Take unto thee sweet spices, stacte, and onycha, and galbanum; sweet spices with pure frankincense; of each shall there be a like weight.

**35.** And thou shalt make of it incense, a perfume after the art of the  perfumer, seasoned with salt, pure and holy.

**36.** And thou shalt beat some of it very small, and put of it before the testimony in the tent of meeting, where I will meet with thee; it shall be unto you most holy.

**37.** And the incense which thou shalt make, according to the composition thereof ye shall not make for yourselves; it shall be unto thee holy for the LORD.

**38.** Whosoever shall make like unto that, to smell thereof, he shall be cut off from his people.

## Chapter 31

**1.** And the LORD spoke unto Moses, saying:

**2.** See, I have called by name Bezalel the son of Uri, the son of Hur, of the tribe of Judah;

**3.** And I have filled him with the spirit of God, in wisdom, and in understanding, and in knowledge, and in all manner of workmanship,

**4.** To devise skilful works, to work in gold, and in silver, and in brass,

**5.** And in cutting of stones for setting, and in carving of wood, to work in all manner of workmanship.

**6.** And I, behold, I have appointed with him Oholiab, the son of Ahisamach, of the tribe of Dan; and in the hearts of all that are wise-hearted I have put wisdom, that they may make all that I have commanded thee:

**7.** The tent of meeting, and the ark of the testimony, and the ark-cover that is thereupon, and all the furniture of the Tent;

**8.** And the table and its vessels, and the pure candlestick with all its vessels, and the altar of incense;

**9.** And the altar of burnt-offering with all its vessels, and the laver and its base;

**10.** And the plaited garments, and the holy garments for Aaron the priest, and the garments of his sons, to minister in the priest's office;

**11.** And the anointing oil, and the incense of sweet spices for the holy place; according to all that I have commanded thee shall they do.

**12.** And the LORD spoke unto Moses, saying:

**13.** Speak thou also unto the children of Israel, saying: Verily ye shall keep My sabbaths, for it is a sign between Me and you throughout your generations, that ye may know that I am the LORD who sanctify you.

**14.** Ye shall keep the sabbath therefore, for it is holy unto you; every one that profaneth it shall surely be put to death; for whosoever doeth any work therein, that soul shall be cut off from among his people.

**15.** Six days shall work be done; but on the seventh day is a sabbath of solemn rest, holy to the LORD; whosoever doeth any work in the sabbath day, he shall surely be put to death.

**16.** Wherefore the children of Israel shall keep the sabbath, to observe the sabbath throughout their generations, for a perpetual covenant.

**17.** It is a sign  between Me and the children of Israel

for ever; for in six days the LORD made heaven and earth, and on the seventh day He ceased from work and rested.

**18.** And He gave unto Moses, when He had made an end of speaking with him upon mount Sinai, the two tables of the testimony, tables of stone, written with the finger of God.

## Chapter 32

**1.** And when the people saw that Moses delayed to come down from the mount, the people gathered themselves together unto Aaron, and said unto him: Up, make us a god who shall go before us; for as for this Moses, the man that brought us up out of the land of Egypt, we know not what is become of him.

**2.** And Aaron said unto them: Break off the golden rings, which are in the ears of your wives, of your sons, and of your daughters, and bring them unto me.

**3.** And all the people broke off the golden rings which were in their ears, and brought them unto Aaron.

**4.** And he received it at their hand, and fashioned it with a graving tool, and made it a molten calf; and they said: This is thy god, O Israel, which brought thee up out of the land of Egypt.

**5.** And when Aaron saw this, he built an altar before it; and Aaron made proclamation, and said: To-morrow shall be a feast to the LORD.

**6.** And they rose up early on the morrow, and offered burnt-offerings, and brought peace-offerings; and the people sat down to eat and to drink, and rose up to make merry.

**7.** And the LORD spoke unto Moses: Go, get thee down; for thy people, that thou broughtest up out of the land of Egypt, have dealt corruptly;

**8.** They have turned aside quickly out of the way which I commanded them; they have made them a molten calf, and have worshipped it, and have sacrificed unto it, and said: This is thy god, O Israel, which brought thee up out of the land of Egypt.

**9.** And the LORD said unto Moses: I have seen this people, and, behold, it is a stiffnecked people.

**10.** Now therefore let Me alone, that My wrath may wax hot against them, and that I may consume them; and I will make of thee a great nation.

**11.** And Moses besought the LORD his God, and said: LORD, why doth Thy wrath wax hot against Thy people, that Thou hast brought forth out of the land of Egypt with great power and with a mighty hand?

**12.** Wherefore should the Egyptians speak, saying: For evil did He bring them forth, to slay them in the mountains, and to consume them from the face of the earth? Turn from Thy fierce wrath, and repent of this evil against Thy people.

**13.** Remember Abraham, Isaac, and Israel, thy servants, to whom Thou didst swear by Thine own self, and saidst unto them: I will multiply your seed as the stars of heaven, and all this land that I have spoken of will I give unto your seed, and they shall inherit it for ever.

**14.** And the LORD repented of the evil which He said He would do unto His people.

**15.** And Moses turned, and went down from the mount, with the two tables of the testimony in his hand; tables that were written on both their sides; on the one side and on the other were they written.

**16.** And the tables were the work of God, and the writing was the writing of God, graven upon the tables.

**17.** And when Joshua heard the noise of the people as they shouted, he said unto Moses: There is a noise of war in the camp.

**18.** And he said: It is not the voice of them that shout for mastery, neither is it the voice of them that cry for being overcome, but the noise of them that sing do I hear.

**19.** And it came to pass, as soon as he came nigh unto the camp, that he saw the calf and the dancing; and Moses' anger waxed hot, and he cast the tables out of his hands, and broke them beneath the mount.

**20.** And he took the calf which they had made, and burnt it with fire, and ground it to powder, and strewed it upon the water, and made the children of Israel drink of it.

**21.** And Moses said unto Aaron: What did this people unto thee, that thou hast brought a great sin upon them?

**22.** And Aaron said: Let not the anger of my lord wax hot; thou knowest the people, that they are set on evil.

**23.** So, they said unto me: Make us a god, which shall go before us; for as for this Moses, the man that brought us up out of the land of Egypt, we know not what is become of him.

**24.** And I said unto them: Whosoever hath any gold, let them break it off; so, they gave it me; and I cast it into the fire, and there came out this calf.

**25.** And when Moses saw that the people were broken loose - for Aaron had let them loose for a derision among their enemies.

**26.** Then Moses stood in the gate of the camp, and said: Whoso is on the LORD'S side, let him come unto me. And all the sons of Levi gathered themselves together unto him.

**27.** And he said unto them: Thus, saith the LORD, the God of Israel: Put  ye  every  man his sword upon his thigh, and go to and fro from gate to gate throughout the camp, and slay every man his brother, and every man his companion, and every man his neighbour.

**28.** And the sons of Levi did according to the word of Moses; and there fell of the people that day about three thousand men.

**29.** And Moses said: Consecrate yourselves to-day to the LORD, for every man hath been against his son and against his brother; that He may also bestow upon you a blessing this day.

**30.** And it came to pass on the morrow, that Moses said unto the people: Ye have sinned a great sin; and now I will go up unto the LORD, peradventure I shall make atonement for your sin.

**31.** And Moses returned unto the LORD, and said: Oh, this people have sinned a great sin, and have made them a god of gold.

**32.** Yet now, if Thou wilt forgive their sin; and if not, blot me, I pray Thee, out of Thy book which Thou hast written.

**33.** And the LORD said unto Moses: Whosoever hath sinned against Me, him will I blot out of My book.

**34.** And now go, lead the people unto the place of which I have spoken unto thee; behold, Mine angel shall go before thee; nevertheless, in the day when I visit, I will visit their sin upon them.

**35.** And the LORD smote the people, because they made the calf, which Aaron made.

## Chapter 33

**1.** And the LORD spoke unto Moses: Depart, go up hence, thou and the people that thou hast brought up out of the land of Egypt, unto the land of which I swore unto Abraham, to Isaac, and to Jacob, saying: Unto thy seed will I give it.

**2.** And I will send an angel before thee; and I will drive out the Canaanite, the Amorite, and the Hittite, and the Perizzite, the Hivite, and the Jebusite.

**3.** Unto a land flowing with milk and honey; for I will

not go up in the midst of thee; for thou art a stiffnecked people; lest I consume thee in the way.

**4.** And when the people heard these evil tidings, they mourned; and no man did put on him his ornaments.

**5.** And the LORD said unto Moses: Say unto the children of Israel: Ye are a stiffnecked people; if I go up into the midst of thee for one moment, I shall consume thee; therefore, now put off thy ornaments from thee, that I may know what to do unto thee.

**6.** And the children of Israel stripped themselves of their ornaments from mount Horeb onward.

**7.** Now Moses used to take the tent and to pitch it without the camp, afar off from the camp; and he called it the tent of meeting. And it came to pass, that every one that sought the LORD went out unto the tent of meeting, which was without the camp.

**8.** And it came to pass, when Moses went out unto the Tent, that all the people rose up, and stood, every man at his tent door, and looked after Moses, until he was gone into the Tent.

**9.** And it came to pass, when Moses entered into the Tent, the pillar of cloud descended, and stood at the door of the Tent; and the LORD spoke with Moses.

**10.** And when all the people saw the pillar of cloud stand at the door of the Tent, all the people rose up and worshipped, every man at his tent door.

**11.** And the LORD spoke unto Moses face to face, as a man speaketh unto his friend. And he would return into the camp; but his minister Joshua, the son of Nun, a young man, departed not out of the Tent.

**12.** And Moses said unto the LORD: See, thou sayest unto me: Bring up this people; and Thou hast not let me know whom Thou wilt send with me. Yet Thou hast said: I know thee by name, and thou hast also found grace in My sight.

**13.** Now therefore, I pray Thee, if I have found grace in Thy sight, show me now Thy ways, that I may know Thee, to the end that I may find grace in Thy sight; and consider that this nation is Thy people.

**14.** And He said: My presence shall go with thee, and I will give thee rest.

**15.** And he said unto Him: If Thy presence go not with me, carry us not up hence.

**16.** For wherein now shall it be known that I have found grace in Thy sight, I and Thy people? is it not in that Thou goest with us, so that we are distinguished, I and Thy people, from all the people that are upon the face of the earth?

**17.** And the LORD said unto Moses: I will do this thing also that thou hast spoken, for thou hast found grace in My sight, and I know thee by name.

**18.** And he said: Show me, I pray Thee, Thy glory.

**19.** And He said: I will make all My goodness pass before thee, and will proclaim the name of the LORD before thee; and I will be gracious to whom I will be gracious, and will show mercy on whom I will show mercy.

**20.** And He said: Thou canst not see My face, for man

shall not see Me and live.

**21.** And the LORD said: Behold, there is a place by Me, and thou shalt stand upon the rock.

**22.** And it shall come to pass, while My glory passeth by, that I will put thee in a cleft of the rock, and will cover thee with My hand until I have passed by.

**23.** And I will take away My hand, and thou shalt see My back; but My face shall not be seen.

## Chapter 34

**1.** And the LORD said unto Moses: Hew thee two tables of stone like unto the first; and I will write upon the tables the words that were on the first tables, which thou didst break.

**2.** And be ready by the morning, and come up in the morning unto mount Sinai, and present thyself there to Me on the top of the mount.

**3.** And no man shall come up with thee, neither let any man be seen throughout all the mount; neither let the flocks nor herds feed before that mount.

**4.** And he hewed two tables of stone like unto the first; and Moses rose up early in the morning, and went up unto mount Sinai, as the LORD had commanded him, and took in his hand two tables of stone.

**5.** And the LORD descended in the cloud, and stood with him there, and proclaimed the name of the LORD.

**6.** And the LORD passed by before him, and

proclaimed: The LORD, the LORD, God, merciful and gracious, long-suffering, and abundant in goodness and truth;

**7.** Keeping mercy unto the thousandth generation, forgiving iniquity and transgression and sin; and that will by no means clear the guilty; visiting the iniquity of the fathers upon the children, and upon the children's children, unto the third and unto the fourth generation.

**8.** And Moses made haste, and bowed his head toward the earth, and worshipped.

**9.** And he said: If now I have found grace in Thy sight, O Lord, let the Lord, I pray Thee, go in the midst of us; for it is a stiffnecked people; and pardon our iniquity and our sin, and take us for Thine inheritance.

**10.** And He said: Behold, I make a covenant; before all thy people I will do marvels, such as have not been wrought in all the earth, nor in any nation; and all the people among which thou art shall see the work of the LORD that I am about to do with thee, that it is tremendous.

**11.** Observe thou that which I am commanding thee this day; behold, I am driving out before thee the Amorite, and the Canaanite, and the Hittite, and the Perizzite, and the Hivite, and the Jebusite.

**12.** Take heed to thyself, lest thou make a covenant with the inhabitants of the land whither thou goest, lest they be for a snare in the midst of thee.

**13.** But ye shall break down their altars, and dash in pieces their pillars, and ye shall cut down their Asherim.

**14.** For thou shalt bow down to no other god; for the LORD, whose name is Jealous, is a jealous God;

**15.** Lest thou make a covenant with the inhabitants of the land, and they go astray after their gods, and do sacrifice unto their gods, and they call thee, and thou eat of their sacrifice;

**16.** And thou take of their daughters unto thy sons, and their daughters go astray after their gods, and make thy sons go astray after their gods.

**17.** Thou shalt make thee no molten gods.

**18.** The feast of unleavened bread shalt thou keep. Seven days thou shalt eat unleavened bread, as I commanded thee, at the time appointed in the month Abib, for in the month Abib thou camest out from Egypt.

**19.** All that openeth the womb is Mine; and of all thy cattle thou shalt sanctify the males, the firstlings of ox and sheep.

**20.** And the firstling of an ass thou shalt redeem with a lamb; and if thou wilt not redeem it, then thou shalt break its neck. All the first-born of thy sons thou shalt redeem. And none shall appear before Me empty.

**21.** Six days thou shalt work, but on the seventh day thou shalt rest; in plowing time and in harvest thou shalt rest.

**22.** And  thou shalt observe the  feast of weeks, even

of the first-fruits of wheat harvest, and the feast of ingathering at the turn of the year.

**23.** Three times in the year shall all thy males appear before the Lord GOD, the God of Israel.

**24.** For I will cast out nations before thee, and enlarge thy borders; neither shall any man covet thy land, when thou goes' up to appear before the LORD thy God three times in the year.

**25.** Thou shalt not offer the blood of My sacrifice with leavened bread; neither shall the sacrifice of the feast of the Passover be left unto the morning.

**26.** The choicest first-fruits of thy land thou shalt bring unto the house of the LORD thy God. Thou shalt not seethe a kid in its mother's milk.

**27.** And the LORD said unto Moses: Write thou these words, for after the tenor of these words I have made a covenant with thee and with Israel.

**28.** And he was there with the LORD forty days and forty nights; he did neither eat bread, nor drink water. And he wrote upon the tables the words of the covenant, the ten words.

**29.** And it came to pass, when Moses came down from mount Sinai with the two tables of the testimony in Moses' hand, when he came down from the mount, that Moses knew not that the skin of his face sent forth abeams while He talked with him.

**30.** And when Aaron and all the children of Israel saw Moses, behold, the skin of his face sent forth beams; and they were afraid to come nigh him.

**31.** And Moses called unto them; and Aaron and all the rulers of the congregation returned unto him; and Moses spoke to them.

**32.** And afterward all the children of Israel came nigh, and he gave them in commandment all that the LORD had spoken with him in mount Sinai.

**33.** And when Moses had done speaking with them, he put a veil on his face.

**34.** But when Moses went in before the LORD that He might speak with him, he took the veil off, until he came out; and he came out; and spoke unto the children of Israel that which he was commanded.

**35.** And the children of Israel saw the face of Moses, that the skin of Moses face sent forth beams; and Moses put the veil back upon his face, until he went in to speak with Him.

### Vayakhel

## Chapter 35

**1.** And Moses assembled all the congregation of the children of Israel, and said unto them: These are the words which the LORD hath commanded, that ye should do them.

**2.** Six days shall work be done, but on the seventh day there shall be to you a holy day, a sabbath of solemn rest to the LORD; whosoever doeth any work therein shall be put to death.

**3.** Ye shall kindle no fire throughout your habitations

upon the sabbath day.

**4.** And Moses spoke unto all the congregation of the children of Israel, saying: This is the thing which the LORD commanded, saying:

**5.** Take ye from among you an offering unto the LORD, whosoever is of a willing heart, let him bring it, the LORD'S offering: gold, and silver, and brass;

**6.** And blue, and purple, and scarlet, and fine linen, and goats' hair;

**7.** And rams' skins dyed red, and sealskins, and acacia-wood;

**8.** And oil for the light, and spices for the anointing oil, and for the sweet incense;

**9.** And onyx stones, and stones to be set, for the ephod, and for the breastplate.

**10.** And let every wise-hearted man among you come, and make all that the LORD hath commanded:

**11.** The tabernacle, its tent, and its covering, its clasps, and its boards, its bars, its pillars, and its sockets;

**12.** The ark, and the staves thereof, the ark-cover, and the veil of the screen;

**13.** The table, and its staves, and all its vessels, and the showbread;

**14.** The candlestick also for the light, and its vessels, and its lamps, and the oil for the light;

**15.** And the altar of incense, and its staves, and the anointing oil, and the sweet incense, and the screen for the door, at the door of the tabernacle;

**16.** The altar of burnt-offering, with its grating of brass, its staves, and all its vessels, the laver and its base;

**17.** The hangings of the court, the pillars thereof, and their sockets, and the screen for the gate of the court;

**18.** The pins of the tabernacle, and the pins of the court, and their cords;

**19.** The plaited garments, for ministering in the holy place, the holy garments for Aaron the priest, and the garments of his sons, to minister in the priest's office.

**20.** And all the congregation of the children of Israel departed from the presence of Moses.

**21.** And they came, every one whose heart stirred him up, and every one whom his spirit made willing, and brought the LORD'S offering, for the work of the tent of meeting, and for all the service thereof, and for the holy garments.

**22.** And they came, both men and women, as many as were willing-hearted, and brought nose-rings, and ear-rings, and signet-rings, and girdles, all jewels of gold; even every man that brought an offering of gold unto the LORD.

**23.** And every man, with whom was found blue, and purple, and scarlet, and fine linen, and goats' hair, and rams' skins dyed red, and sealskins, brought them.

**24.** Every one that did set apart an offering of silver and brass brought the LORD'S offering; and every man, with whom was found acacia-wood for any work of the service, brought it.

**25.** And all the women that were wise-hearted did spin with their hands, and brought that which they had spun, the blue, and the purple, the scarlet, and the fine linen.

**26.** And all the women whose heart stirred them up in wisdom spun the goats' hair.

**27.** And the rulers brought the onyx stones, and the stones to be set, for the ephod, and for the breastplate;

**28.** And the spice, and the oil, for the light, and for the anointing oil, and for the sweet incense.

**29.** The children of Israel brought a freewill-offering unto the LORD; every man and woman, whose heart made them willing to bring for all the work, which the LORD had commanded by the hand of Moses to be made.

**30.** And Moses said unto the children of Israel: See, the LORD hath called by name Bezalel the son of Uri, the son of Hur, of the tribe of Judah.

**31.** And He hath filled him with the spirit of God, in wisdom, in understanding, and in knowledge, and in all manner of workmanship.

**32.** And to devise skilful works, to work in gold, and in silver, and in brass,

**33.** And in cutting of stones for setting, and in carving of wood, to work in all manner of skilful workmanship.

**34.** And He hath put in his heart that he may teach, both he, and Oholiab, the son of Ahisamach, of the tribe of Dan.

**35.** Them hath He filled with wisdom of heart, to work all manner of workmanship, of the craftsman, and of the skilful workman, and of the weaver in colours, in blue, and in purple, in scarlet, and in fine linen, and of the weaver, even of them that do any workmanship, and of those that devise skilful works.

## Chapter 36

**1.** And Bezalel and Oholiab shall work, and every wise-hearted man, in whom the LORD hath put wisdom and understanding to know how to work all the work for the service of the sanctuary, according to all that the LORD hath commanded.

**2.** And Moses called Bezalel and Oholiab, and every wise-hearted man, in whose heart the LORD had put wisdom, even every one whose heart stirred him up to come unto the work to do it.

**3.** And they received of Moses all the offering, which the children of Israel had brought for the work of the service of the sanctuary, wherewith to make it. And they brought yet unto him freewill-offerings every morning.

**4.** And all the wise men, that wrought all the work of the sanctuary, came every man from his work which they wrought.

**5.** And they spoke unto Moses, saying: The people bring much more than enough for the service of the work, which the LORD commanded to make.

**6.** And Moses gave commandment, and they caused

it to be proclaimed throughout the camp, saying: Let neither man nor woman make any more work for the offering of the sanctuary. So, the people were restrained from bringing.

**7.** For the stuff they had was sufficient for all the work to make it, and too much.

**8.** And every wise-hearted man among them that wrought the work made the tabernacle with ten curtains: of fine twined linen, and blue, and purple, and scarlet, with cherubim the work of the skilful workman made he them.

**9.** The length of each curtain was eight and twenty cubits, and the breadth of each curtain four cubits; all the curtains had one measure.

**10.** And he coupled five curtains one to another; and the other five curtains he coupled one to another.

**11.** And he made loops of blue upon the edge of the one curtain that was outmost in the first set; likewise, he made in the edge of the curtain that was outmost in the second set.

**12.** Fifty loops made he in the one curtain, and fifty loops made he in the edge of the curtain that was in the second set; the loops were opposite one to another.

**13.** And he made fifty clasps of gold, and coupled the curtains one to another with the clasps; so the tabernacle was one.

**14.** And he made curtains of goats' hair for a tent over the tabernacle; eleven curtains he made them.

**15.** The length of each curtain was thirty cubits, and four cubits the breadth of each curtain; the eleven curtains had one measure.

**16.** And he coupled five curtains by themselves, and six curtains by themselves.

**17.** And he made fifty loops on the edge of the curtain that was outmost in the first set, and fifty loops made he upon the edge of the curtain which was outmost in the second set.

**18.** And he made fifty clasps of brass to couple the tent together, that it might be one.

**19.** And he made a covering for the tent of rams' skins dyed red, and a covering of sealskins above.

**20.** And he made the boards for the tabernacle of acacia-wood, standing up.

**21.** Ten cubits was the length of a board, and a cubit and a half the breadth of each board.

**22.** Each board had two tenons, joined one to another. Thus, did he make for all the boards of the tabernacle.

**23.** And he made the boards for the tabernacle; twenty boards for the south side southward.

**24.** And he made forty sockets of silver under the twenty boards: two sockets under one board for its two tenons, and two sockets under another board for its two tenons.

**25.** And for the second side of the tabernacle, on the north side, he made twenty boards,

**26.** And their forty sockets of silver: two sockets under one board, and two sockets under another board.

**27.** And for the hinder part of the tabernacle westward he made six boards.

**28.** And two boards made he for the corners of the tabernacle in the hinder part;

**29.** That they might be double beneath, and in like manner they should be complete unto the top thereof unto the first ring. Thus, he did to both of them in the two corners.

**30.** And there were eight boards, and their sockets of silver, sixteen sockets: under every board two sockets.

**31.** And he made bars of acacia-wood: five for the boards of the one side of the tabernacle,

**32.** And five bars for the boards of the other side of the tabernacle, and five bars for the boards of the tabernacle for the hinder part westward.

**33.** And he made the middle bar to pass through in the midst of the boards from the one end to the other.

**34.** And he overlaid the boards with gold, and made their rings of gold for holders for the bars, and overlaid the bars with gold.

**35.** And he made the veil of blue, and purple, and scarlet, and fine twined linen; with the cherubim the work of the skilful workman made he it.

**36.** And he made thereunto four pillars of acacia, and overlaid them with gold, their hooks being of gold; and he cast for them four sockets of silver.

**37.** And he made a screen for the door of the Tent, of

blue, and purple, and scarlet, and fine twined linen, the work of the weaver in colours;

**38.** And the five pillars of it with their hooks; and he overlaid their capitals and their fillets with gold; and their five sockets were of brass.


## Chapter 37

**1.** And Bezalel made the ark of acacia-wood: two cubits and a half was the length of it, and a cubit and a half the breadth of it, and a cubit and a half the height of it.

**2.** And he overlaid it with pure gold within and without, and made a crown of gold to it round about.

**3.** And he cast for it four rings of gold, in the four feet thereof: even two rings on the one side of it, and two rings on the other side of it.

**4.** And he made staves of acacia-wood, and overlaid them with gold.

**5.** And he put the staves into the rings on the sides of the ark, to bear the ark.

**6.** And he made an ark-cover of pure gold: two cubits and a half was the length thereof, and a cubit and a half the breadth thereof.

**7.** And he made two cherubim of gold: of beaten work made he them, at the two ends of the ark-cover:

**8.** One cherub at the one end, and one cherub at the other end; of one piece with the ark-cover made he the cherubim at the two ends thereof.

**9.** And the  cherubim spread  out their wings on high,

screening the ark-cover with their wings, with their faces one to another; toward the ark-cover were the faces of the cherubim.

**10.** And he made the table of acacia-wood: two cubits was the length thereof, and a cubit the breadth thereof, and a cubit and a half the height thereof.

**11.** And he overlaid it with pure gold, and made thereto a crown of gold round about.

**12.** And he made unto it a border of a hand-breadth round about, and made a golden crown to the border thereof round about.

**13.** And he cast for it four rings of gold, and put the rings in the four corners that were on the four feet thereof.

**14.** Close by the border were the rings, the holders for the staves to bear the table.

**15.** And he made the staves of acacia-wood, and overlaid them with gold, to bear the table.

**16.** And he made the vessels which were upon the table, the dishes thereof, and the pans thereof, and the bowls thereof, and the jars thereof, wherewith to pour out, of pure gold.

**17.** And he made the candlestick of pure gold: of beaten work made he the candlestick, even its base, and its shaft; its cups, its knops, and its flowers, were of one piece with it.

**18.** And there were six branches going out of the sides thereof: three branches of the candlestick out of the one side thereof, and three branches of the candlestick out of the other side thereof;

**19.** Three cups made like almond-blossoms in one branch, a knop and a flower; and three cups made like almond-blossoms in the other branch, a knop and a flower. So, for the six branches going out of the candlestick.

**20.** And in the candlestick were four cups made like almond-blossoms, the knops thereof, and the flowers thereof;

**21.** And a knop under two branches of one piece with it, and a knop under two branches of one piece with it, and a knop under two branches of one piece with it, for the six branches going out of it.

**22.** Their knops and their branches were of one piece with it; the whole of it was one beaten work of pure gold.

**23.** And he made the lamps thereof, seven, and the tongs thereof, and the snuffdishes thereof, of pure gold.

**24.** Of a talent of pure gold made he it, and all the vessels thereof.

**25.** And he made the altar of incense of acacia-wood: a cubit was the length thereof, and a cubit the breadth thereof, four-square; and two cubits was the height thereof; the horns thereof were of one piece with it.

**26.** And he overlaid it with pure gold, the top thereof, and the sides thereof round about, and the horns of it; and he made unto it a crown of gold round about.

**27.** And  he  made  for it two golden rings under the

crown thereof, upon the two ribs thereof, upon the two sides of it, for holders for staves wherewith to bear it.

**28.** And he made the staves of acacia-wood, and overlaid them with gold.

**29.** And he made the holy anointing oil, and the pure incense of sweet spices, after the art of the perfumer.

## Chapter 38

**1.** And he made the altar of burnt-offering of acacia-wood: five cubits was the length thereof, and five cubits the breadth thereof, four-square, and three cubits the height thereof.

**2.** And he made the horns thereof upon the four corners of it; the horns thereof were of one piece with it; and he overlaid it with brass.

**3.** And he made all the vessels of the altar, the pots, and the shovels, and the basins, the flesh-hooks, and the fire-pans; all the vessels thereof made he of brass.

**4.** And he made for the altar a grating of network of brass, under the ledge round it beneath, reaching halfway up.

**5.** And he cast four rings for the four ends of the grating of brass, to be holders for the staves.

**6.** And he made the staves of acacia-wood, and overlaid them with brass.

**7.** And he put the staves into the rings on the sides of the altar, wherewith to bear it; he made it hollow with planks.

**8.** And he made the laver of brass, and the base thereof of brass, of the mirrors of the serving women that did service at the door of the tent of meeting.

**9.** And he made the court; for the south side southward the hangings of the court were of fine twined linen, a hundred cubits.

**10.** Their pillars were twenty, and their sockets twenty, of brass; the hooks of the pillars and their fillets were of silver.

**11.** And for the north side a hundred cubits, their pillars twenty, and their sockets twenty, of brass; the hooks of the pillars and their fillets of silver.

**12.** And for the west side were hangings of fifty cubits, their pillars ten, and their sockets ten; the hooks of the pillars and their fillets of silver.

**13.** And for the east side eastward fifty cubits.

**14.** The hangings for the one side [of the gate] were fifteen cubits; their pillars three, and their sockets three.

**15.** And so, for the other side; on this hand and that hand by the gate of the court were hangings of fifteen cubits; their pillars three, and their sockets three.

**16.** All the hangings of the court round about were of fine twined linen.

**17.** And the sockets for the pillars were of brass; the hooks of the pillars and their fillets of silver; and the overlaying of their capitals of silver; and all the pillars of the court were filleted with silver.

**18.** And  the screen  for the gate of the court was the

work of the weaver in colours, of blue, and purple, and scarlet, and fine twined linen; and twenty cubits was the length, and the height in the breadth was five cubits, answerable to the hangings of the court.

**19.** And their pillars were four, and their sockets four of brass; their hooks of silver, and the overlaying of their capitals and their fillets of silver.

**20.** And all the pins of the tabernacle, and of the court round about, were of brass.

## Pekudei

**21.** These are the accounts of the tabernacle, even the tabernacle of the testimony, as they were rendered according to the commandment of Moses, through the service of the Levites, by the hand of Ithamar, the son of Aaron the priest.

**22.** And Bezalel the son of Uri, the son of Hur, of the tribe of Judah, made all that the LORD commanded Moses.

**23.** And with him was Oholiab, the son of Ahisamach, of the tribe of Dan, a craftsman, and a skilful workman, and a weaver in colours, in blue, and in purple, and in scarlet, and fine linen.

**24.** All the gold that was used for the work in all the work of the sanctuary, even the gold of the offering, was twenty and nine talents, and seven hundred and thirty shekels, after the shekel of the sanctuary.

**25.** And the silver of them that were numbered of the

congregation was a hundred talents, and a thousand seven hundred and three-score and fifteen shekels, after the shekel of the sanctuary:

**26.** A beka a head, that is, half a shekel, after the shekel of the sanctuary, for every one that passed over to them that are numbered, from twenty years old and upward, for six hundred thousand and three thousand and five hundred and fifty men.

**27.** And the hundred talents of silver were for casting the sockets of the sanctuary, and the sockets of the veil: a hundred sockets for the hundred talents, a talent for a socket.

**28.** And of the thousand seven hundred seventy and five shekels he made hooks for the pillars, and overlaid their capitals, and made fillets for them.

**29.** And the brass of the offering was seventy talents and two thousand and four hundred shekels.

**30.** And therewith he made the sockets to the door of the tent of meeting, and the brazen altar, and the brazen grating for it, and all the vessels of the altar,

**31.** And the sockets of the court round about, and the sockets of the gate of the court, and all the pins of the tabernacle, and all the pins of the court round about.

## Chapter 39

**1.** And of the blue, and purple, and scarlet, they made plaited garments, for ministering in the holy place, and made the holy   garments for Aaron, as the LORD commanded Moses.

**2.** And he made the ephod of gold, blue, and purple, and scarlet, and fine twined linen.

**3.** And they did beat the gold into thin plates, and cut it into threads, to work it in the blue, and in the purple, and in the scarlet, and in the fine linen, the work of the skilful workman.

**4.** They made shoulder-pieces for it, joined together; at the two ends was it joined together.

**5.** And the skilfully woven band, that was upon it, wherewith to gird it on, was of the same piece and like the work thereof: of gold, of blue, and purple, and scarlet, and fine twined linen, as the LORD commanded Moses.

**6.** And they wrought the onyx stones, inclosed in settings of gold, graven with the engravings of a signet, according to the names of the children of Israel.

**7.** And he put them on the shoulder-pieces of the ephod, to be stones of memorial for the children of Israel, as the LORD commanded Moses.

**8.** And he made the breastplate, the work of the skilful workman, like the work of the ephod: of gold, of blue, and purple, and scarlet, and fine twined linen.

**9.** It was four-square; they made the breastplate double; a span was the length thereof, and a span the breadth thereof, being double.

**10.** And they set in it four rows of stones: a row of carnelian, topaz, and smaragd was the first row.

**11.** And the second row, a carbuncle, a sapphire, and an emerald.

**12.** And the third row, a jacinth, an agate, and an amethyst.

**13.** And the fourth row, a beryl, an onyx, and a jasper; they were inclosed in fittings of gold in their settings.

**14.** And the stones were according to the names of the children of Israel, twelve, according to their names, like the engravings of a signet, every one according to his name, for the twelve tribes.

**15.** And they made upon the breastplate plaited chains, of wreathen work of pure gold.

**16.** And they made two settings of gold, and two gold rings; and put the two rings on the two ends of the breastplate.

**17.** And they put the two wreathen chains of gold on the two rings at the ends of the breastplate.

**18.** And the other two ends of the two wreathen chains they put on the two settings, and put them on the shoulder-pieces of the ephod, in the forepart thereof.

**19.** And they made two rings of gold, and put them upon the two ends of the breastplate, upon the edge thereof, which was toward the side of the ephod inward.

**20.** And they made two rings of gold, and put them on the two shoulder-pieces of the ephod underneath, in the forepart thereof, close by the coupling thereof, above the skilfully woven band of the ephod.

**21.** And they did bind the breastplate by the rings thereof unto the rings of the ephod with a thread of blue, that it might be upon the skilfully woven band of the ephod, and that the breastplate might not be loosed from the ephod; as the LORD commanded Moses.

**22.** And he made the robe of the ephod of woven work, all of blue;

**23.** And the hole of the robe in the midst thereof, as the hole of a coat of mail, with a binding round about the hole of it, that it should not be rent.

**24.** And they made upon the skirts of the robe pomegranates of blue, and purple, and scarlet, and twined linen.

**25.** And they made bells of pure gold, and put the bells between the pomegranates upon the skirts of the robe round about, between the pomegranates:

**26.** A bell and a pomegranate, a bell and a pomegranate, upon the skirts of the robe round about, to minister in; as the LORD commanded Moses.

**27.** And they made the tunics of fine linen of woven work for Aaron, and for his sons,

**28.** And the mitre of fine linen, and the goodly head-tires of fine linen, and the linen breeches of fine twined linen,

**29.** And the girdle of fine twined linen, and blue, and purple, and scarlet, the work of the weaver in colours; as the LORD commanded Moses.

**30.** And they made the plate of the hol crown of pure

gold, and wrote upon it a writing, like the engravings of a signet: HOLY TO THE LORD.

**31.** And they tied unto it a thread of blue, to fasten it upon the mitre above; as the LORD commanded Moses.

**32.** Thus, was finished all the work of the tabernacle of the tent of meeting; and the children of Israel did according to all that the LORD commanded Moses, so did they.

**33.** And they brought the tabernacle unto Moses, the Tent, and all its furniture, its clasps, its boards, its bars, and its pillars, and its sockets;

**34.** And the covering of rams' skins dyed red, and the covering of sealskins, and the veil of the screen;

**35.** The ark of the testimony, and the staves thereof, and the ark-cover;

**36.** The table, all the vessels thereof, and the showbread;

**37.** The pure candlestick, the lamps thereof, even the lamps to be set in order, and all the vessels thereof, and the oil for the light;

**38.** And the golden altar, and the anointing oil, and the sweet incense, and the screen for the door of the Tent;

**39.** The brazen altar, and its grating of brass, its staves, and all its vessels, the laver and its base;

**40.** The hangings of the court, its pillars, and its sockets, and the screen for the gate of the court, the cords thereof, and the pins thereof, and all the instruments of the service of the tabernacle of the tent of meeting;

**41.** The plaited garments for ministering in the holy place; the holy garments for Aaron the priest, and the garments of his sons, to minister in the priest's office.

**42.** According to all that the LORD commanded Moses, so the children of Israel did all the work.

**43.** And Moses saw all the work, and, behold, they had done it; as the LORD had commanded, even so had they done it. And Moses blessed them.

## Chapter 40

**1.** And the LORD spoke unto Moses, saying:

**2.** On the first day of the first month shalt thou rear up the tabernacle of the tent of meeting.

**3.** And thou shalt put therein the ark of the testimony, and thou shalt screen the ark with the veil.

**4.** And thou shalt bring in the table, and set in order the bread that is upon it; and thou shalt bring in the candlestick, and light the lamps thereof.

**5.** And thou shalt set the golden altar for incense before the ark of the testimony, and put the screen of the door to the tabernacle.

**6.** And thou shalt set the altar of burnt-offering before the door of the tabernacle of the tent of meeting.

**7.** And thou shalt set the laver between the tent of meeting and the altar, and shalt put water therein.

**8.** And thou shalt set up the court round about, and hang up the screen of the gate of the court.

**9.** And thou shalt take the anointing oil, and anoint the tabernacle, and all that is therein, and shalt hallow it, and all the furniture thereof; and it shall be holy.

**10.** And thou shalt anoint the altar of burnt-offering, and all its vessels, and sanctify the altar; and the altar shall be most holy.

**11.** And thou shalt anoint the laver and its base, and sanctify it.

**12.** And thou shalt bring Aaron and his sons unto the door of the tent of meeting, and shalt wash them with water.

**13.** And thou shalt put upon Aaron the holy garments; and thou shalt anoint him, and sanctify him, that he may minister unto Me in the priest's office.

**14.** And thou shalt bring his sons, and put tunics upon them.

**15.** And thou shalt anoint them, as thou didst anoint their father, that they may minister unto Me in the priest's office; and their anointing shall be to them for an everlasting priesthood throughout their generations.

**16.** Thus did Moses; according to all that the LORD commanded him, so did he.

**17.** And it came to pass in the first month in the second year, on the first day of the month, that the tabernacle was reared up.

**18.** And Moses reared up the tabernacle, and laid its sockets, and set up the boards thereof, and put in the bars thereof, and reared up its pillars.

**19.** And he spread the tent over the tabernacle, and put the covering of the tent above upon it; as the LORD commanded Moses.

**20.** And he took and put the testimony into the ark, and set the staves on the ark, and put the ark-cover above upon the ark.

**21.** And he brought the ark into the tabernacle, and set up the veil of the screen, and screened the ark of the testimony; as the LORD commanded Moses.

**22.** And he put the table in the tent of meeting, upon the side of the tabernacle northward, without the veil.

**23.** And he set a row of bread in order upon it before the LORD; as the LORD commanded Moses.

**24.** And he put the candlestick in the tent of meeting, over against the table, on the side of the tabernacle southward.

**25.** And he lighted the lamps before the LORD; as the LORD commanded Moses.

**26.** And he put the golden altar in the tent of meeting before the veil;

**27.** And he burnt thereon incense of sweet spices; as the LORD commanded Moses.

**28.** And he put the screen of the door to the tabernacle.

**29.** And the altar of burnt-offering he set at the door of the tabernacle of the tent of meeting, and offered upon it the burnt-offering and the meal-offering; as the LORD commanded Moses.

**30.** And he set the laver  between the tent  of meeting

and the altar, and put water therein, wherewith to wash;

**31.** That Moses and Aaron and his sons might wash their hands and their feet threat;

**32.** When they went into the tent of meeting, and when they came near unto the altar, they should wash; as the LORD commanded Moses.

**33.** And he reared up the court round about the tabernacle and the altar, and set up the screen of the gate of the court. So, Moses finished the work.

**34.** Then the cloud covered the tent of meeting, and the glory of the LORD filled the tabernacle.

**35.** And Moses was not able to enter into the tent of meeting, because the cloud abode thereon, and the glory of the LORD filled the tabernacle.

**36.** And whenever the cloud was taken up from over the tabernacle, the children of Israel went onward, throughout all their journeys.

**37.** But if the cloud was not taken up, then they journeyed not till the day that it was taken up.

**38.** For the cloud of the LORD was upon the tabernacle by day, and there was fire therein by night, in the sight of all the house of Israel, throughout all their journeys.